Job 'Creation'—
OR DESTRUCTION?

Job 'Creation'— or DESTRUCTION?

Six essays on the effects of government intervention in the labour market

JOHN ADDISON □ CHRISTIAN WATRIN

MALCOLM R. FISHER □ ALBERT REES

YUKIHIDE OKANO and MITSUAKI OKABE

WALTER ELTIS

With an Introductory Essay by
RALPH HARRIS

Published by
The Institute of Economic Affairs
1979

First published in August 1979 by
THE INSTITUTE OF ECONOMIC AFFAIRS
© The Institute of Economic Affairs 1979

ISBN 0305-814X
ISBN 0-255 36121-1

Printed in England by
Eastbourne Printers Limited, Eastbourne, East Sussex
Set in Monotype Times Roman 11 on 12 point

Contents

v

Contents

Contents

Preface

The *IEA Readings* have been devised to refine the market in economic thinking by presenting varying approaches to a single theme in one volume. They are intended primarily for teachers and students of economics but are edited to help non-economists in industry and government who want to know how economics can explain the activities with which they are concerned.

Readings 20 comprises essays by six economists based on papers delivered in December 1978. They concern a subject that it may be thought would hardly require a day-long seminar in which some 18,000 words were spoken by the six speakers and a further 14,000 words were delivered in questions and answers and discussion after each paper. Adam Smith would turn in his grave to learn that the subject of 'job creation' would have to be taken seriously by economists for no better reason than that it has been made a main plank in the policy of government. The father of economics who wrote that the 'sole end and purpose of all production is consumption' produced a new social science which taught that 'jobs' were of value only where they produced goods or services desired by consumers, even if in anticipation of demand. The clear lesson that politicians have difficulty in grasping is that jobs should be 'created' only by the decision of consumers. The task would then be to create the institutions within which consumers could best make their preferences known and heeded. How far these institutions are those of the market or could be created by government is thus the subject of the Seminar.

Unfortunately, 'job creation' was given some intellectual respectability by J. M. Keynes who conceived the possibility that digging holes and filling them could be 'socially useful' in conditions of unemployment because they might indirectly generate demand for the products of other workers and thus 'create' jobs that would otherwise not exist. But this theoretical proposition has been taken to the opposite extreme by government in the years before 1979. Government spokesmen seemed to think it was a self-evident proposition that action to 'create' jobs was desirable and that industrial change that destroyed jobs was undesirable. It is to these issues that the six papers in these minar addressed themselves: essentially whether, in the act of creating jobs, government does not destroy even more; hence the title of the *Readings*.

xi

Job 'Creation'—or Destruction?

The seminar was opened by the Chairman, Mr Ralph Harris, who reviewed some of the essentials of economic thought that bore on the subject. The use of scarce labour resources was a task that faced economies of all kinds, but it was only a market economy that could create market institutions in which an efficient distribution of labour, interpreted as responding to consumer preferences, could be reconciled with the ability of workers of all kinds to stay in or move to preferred employments. Even then the two objectives of efficiency and liberty were often frustrated by government, as when it has tried to control the prices of manufacturers, or restrict housing rents, or subsidise agriculture. The result was to distort the signals created by relative wage-rates, salaries, or other forms of remuneration, and thus to raise the 'natural' rate of unemployment that was compatible with an uncoerced, mobile labour force in an open market. And the solution was to encourage mobility between occupations and regions by retraining, by reducing barriers, and by encouraging mobility through more efficient 'job centres' (where government labour exchanges could learn from private employment agencies).

Not least, Mr Harris pointed to the ability of the market in the long run to find ways round restrictions by trade unions or by government itself. Industries in which costs were kept unnecessarily high by 'preserving' jobs, or in which jobs 'created' by government produced goods that would not sell, would find that capital tended to escape to other industries where job creation was less oppressive or, in the last resort, to other countries. The emigration of industry is the last-resort exit from over-restrictive government that could increase as the Common Market and the world economy develop, in more liberal directions.

In the opening paper Dr John Addison of the University of Aberdeen began with a general discussion of the economics of job creation by subsidy; he asked whether they worked, and, if they did, whether they were nevertheless wise.

Professor Malcolm Fisher of the University of New South Wales spoke about the function of differentials and relativities in inducing movement of labour between occupations and industries to make more optimal use of it. His paper was followed by others from economists in three countries with whose labour markets unfavourable comparisons are usually drawn when discussing the British labour market. Professor Albert Rees of Princeton University spoke of aspects of the labour market in the USA, especially the effects of

xii

trade unions on productivity; Professor Yukihide Okano of Tokyo University discussed the use of labour in Japanese industry; and Professor Christian Watrin of the University of Cologne analysed recent thinking and practice in West Germany on the efficient use of its labour force.

The discussions were reviewed by Mr Walter Eltis of Oxford who added his interpretation of the main difficulty in Britain—the growth of the non-productive government sector.

Even where there is a plausible macro-economic case for 'job creation' on the ground that it might maintain a higher level of employment than would otherwise exist, its supporters have ignored the probability that the jobs would not be allowed to 'de-create' themselves when the macro-economic circumstances changed. The case for 'job creation' is still argued in Keynesian terms with no recognition of the more recent development of the economics of politics which indicates a much more sceptical judgement about the possibility of using 'job creation' as a delicate instrument to off-set fluctuations in employment. But, much more important, 'job creation' is in essence a device created by government to justify its failure to resist the obstacles to the reconstruction of industry made desirable by changes in the underlying conditions of supply and demand. Its most ironic expression is the Manpower Services Commission whose activities will be analysed in the future as embodying the fallacy adumbrated by Adam Smith 200 years ago.

The texts in this *Readings* are offered as shedding light by clear economic thinking on a subject that has been clouded by intellectual sophistry and political expediency.

I have to thank colleagues for editing the typescript on the question and discussion sessions.

May 1979   ARTHUR SELDON

Introductory Remarks

RALPH HARRIS
Seminar Chairman

The Author

RALPH HARRIS: Lecturer in Political Economy at St Andrews University, 1949-56, and General Director of the Institute of Economic Affairs since 1957. He wrote (with Arthur Seldon) *Hire Purchase in a Free Society, Advertising in a Free Society, Choice in Welfare*, etc., for the IEA. His essay, 'In Place of Incomes Policy', was published in *Catch '76* . . . *?* (Occasional Paper 'Special' (No. 47), 1976). His most recent works, written with Arthur Seldon, are *Pricing or Taxing?* (Hobart Paper No. 71, 1976); *Not from Benevolence* . . . (Hobart Paperback No. 10, 1977) and *Over-Ruled on Welfare* (Hobart Paperback No. 13, 1979); and he contributed the Epilogue, 'Can Confrontation be Avoided?', to *The Coming Confrontation* (Hobart Paperback No. 12, 1978).

Ralph Harris was created a Life Peer in July 1979 as Lord Harris of High Cross.

Since the unemployed are not represented, let me start with a word on their behalf. I do not wish to indulge in the extravagant sentiments characteristic of many politicians—particularly when in opposition and attacking the Government of the day. But it must be acknowledged that the plight of a man or woman genuinely but vainly seeking fulfilment in paid work, over many months, must be deeply depressing. Those of us—at the IEA and elsewhere—who complain of having too much to do are surely to be envied compared with the hundreds of thousands who now seem condemned to indefinite periods of involuntary idleness. A number much smaller than the inflated 1½ million of the official statistics should be enough to cause us all concern—and to lend urgency to our discussions today.

Here, as so often, the humane anxiety of thoughtful laymen is in sympathy with the concern of liberal economists—so often wrongly scorned as hard-boiled, if not hard-hearted.

The preoccupation of economists, after all, is with making scarce resources go as far as possible in catering for the unlimited demands upon them. And since labour in all its forms is the principal resource —accounting ultimately for perhaps 80-85 per cent of all costs of production—the existence of a large army of involuntarily unemployed people mocks our efforts to maximise output as a contribution to economic and social welfare.

Freedom of choice and efficient production=free markets
But for the liberal economist, especially, freedom of choice for both consumers and producers is a value in its own right—as well as a means to efficient production: production not of any old output, nor even of marketable output, but of goods and services whose relative prices reflect as nearly as possible what Marshall described as

> 'the positive motives of desire for different goods, and the negative motives of unwillingness to undergo the fatigues and sacrifices involved in producing them'.

In a free society, there is only one mechanism that is capable in principle of resolving this central problem of the valuation of relative costs of production and relative benefits of consumption. That mechanism is the market.

We know from our standard analysis that where supply and demand are free from constraints, prices tend spontaneously towards a market-clearing level where the quantity freely offered equals the

3

quantity willingly taken up. We know, of course, that competitive markets work optimally only in a deliberately-contrived legal and institutional framework. We also know that at best markets work imperfectly, especially in an open economy characterised by unforeseen and unforeseeable changes in conditions of supply and demand.

But some of us—alas, not yet all—know in addition that governmental policies, even when intended to improve markets, often end up making them work worse. And we should all know that when governments try to operate directly on prices, they disrupt the market's natural tendency towards equilibrium. Thus in the housing market and in the Common Agricultural Policy of the EEC, we have experienced the opposing banes of shortages and surpluses caused by setting administered prices too low (in rents) and too high (in farm products).

So to help clear the ground for our distinguished guest speakers, I have been asked to offer a brief review of the market analysis within which the phenomenon of unemployment can arise to mock the economist's characteristic concern with scarce human (and other) resources. As a proud student of D. H. (Sir Dennis) Robertson, I shall not apologise if my words sometimes recall the spirit of what he used to present as the reflections of an idiot for the benefit of fellow-idiots. My formal paper is entitled: 'Where Does Unemployment Come From?'.

Where Does Unemployment Come From?

RALPH HARRIS

The causes of unemployment are no doubt many and their importance subject to variation from time to time. One more or less constant element in the official statistics is accounted for by about a quarter-of-a-million people who are *unemployable*—in the sense that what an official report called their 'mental and physical condition' makes them unsuited to regular employment at any price.

A growing element is *voluntary* unemployment which, in economists' jargon, arises when individuals judge the net disutility of labour exceeds the net advantages of taking a job. There can be no doubt that, as the demand-price offered the jobless in the form of social benefits has risen, the supply of voluntary unemployment has predictably followed suit. A year ago, when the Government was fighting the firemen over a 10 per cent wage increase, all social benefits were raised by 14½ per cent to cover the rise in the cost of living. Last month (November 1978), when the norm had been brought down to 5 per cent, social benefits were further increased by over 11 per cent.

A number of further elements are lumped together in the broad category of *involuntary* unemployment due to immobility. A crude distinction may be made between geographical and occupational mobility, although it is not always possible precisely to distinguish the two. Furthermore, apparent immobility may be due not so much to unwillingness to move as to ignorance of unfilled vacancies in other trades or areas.

Insofar as these characteristics are a stable part of the social and institutional environment in which the labour market operates, they may be said to help determine what monetarists have called 'the natural rate of unemployment', that is, the minimum rate consistent with zero (or constant) inflation. If we wish to reduce this natural rate the appropriate policies would aim:

first, to facilitate occupational mobility by encouraging the acquisition of new skills through retraining programmes and by reducing such barriers to entry as outdated apprenticeship requirements imposed by trade unions;

second, to encourage geographical mobility by reducing such impediments to moving as rent restriction and council housing;

5

and, *third*, to combat ignorance by extending market information, for example, by infusing 'free' and ineffective Job Centres with something of the vigour displayed by competing private employment agencies that charge for their more effective placement services.

Keynes, Friedman, Hayek

We do not have to be Keynesians to allow that a further 'unnatural' element of unemployment may be associated with the volume of aggregate demand. But where Keynesians argue that persistent unemployment may be caused by chronic deficiency of demand, Friedmanites and other monetarists claim that demand-caused unemployment is a transitional phenomenon which arises from a declining rate of inflation. This effect works through falsifying widely-held expectations that increased costs from an earlier period could be fully recouped from prices continuing to rise at the previous rate. Hayek would insist that inflation distorts pay differentials and makes more and more jobs dependent on its continuance or even acceleration. Therefore, as inflation is checked, many more square pegs fall out of round holes in the labour market.

Turning back to the macro-level, monetarists argue, in contrast to Keynesians, that once the monetary aggregates are stabilised—so that after the appropriate lag inflation is stopped or maintained at a constant rate—no part of the prevailing unemployment can be attributed to demand deficiency. In short, they deny that a lasting gain in employment can be achieved by a once-for-all increase in total monetary demand. On this reckoning, the depth of the pre-war slump was caused by the over-valued sterling exchange rate and the accompanying monetary contraction.

Moving from macro- to more congenial micro-variables, both Keynesians and monetarists must agree that, with any given amount of demand, it is always possible for workers to price themselves—or their fellow workers—out of jobs by insisting on a wage above the value of their contribution to output. The history of minimum wage laws in the USA (and in Britain) confirms this deduction from elementary market analysis. Economists will recall the central problem associated with the textbook theory of wages. We start confidently from the universal law of diminishing marginal returns. This tells us that the additional output from increasing the quantity of any one factor of production rises to a maximum at some point, after which it declines. The practical difficulty for measuring marginal product is that labour is generally employed in more or less fixed combination with capital, so that the net output attributable to work cannot be precisely disentangled from the net output attributable to investment. But it is a truism that there must be a finite limit to the amount wage costs can take from the joint product of capital and labour without reducing the demand for labour in the firm or industry. (It should be emphasised that 'wage costs' include a growing element of other expenses paid by the employer: National Insurance, employment 'protection', holidays, safety and social facilities.)

Labour's short-term gains where investors can escape
Even if we hold to the assumption that productivity remains unchanged, it cannot be denied that labour may for a time gain at the expense of profits. But the share of wages can increase only up to the stage where investors withdraw their co-operation by consuming their capital or by seeking alternative outlets for future investment at home or, if possible, abroad. When the scope for squeezing profits has reached this limit, an increase in wage costs reduces demand for labour through two analytically separable responses. The first is a movement up the demand curve as the number employed is reduced to the point where the higher product of the new marginal worker equals the higher wage. The second, longer-term response to higher wages is a lowering of the entire demand curve as the decline in profits reduces the supply of capital and enterprise. Both effects reduce present and prospective employment below the previous volume. This process has been witnessed at various stages of development in British shipbuilding, motor cars, docks and newspapers.

What of the politician's alibi that increased wages (only) cause inflation? So long as the rate of increase in the money supply does not rise to accommodate the over-pricing of labour—which would simply have the effect of shrinking the value of money and therefore the real cost of higher money wages—the ineluctable effect of pushing wages above the marginal product of labour must be to increase unemployment. The Government led by Mr Callaghan, like its predecessor under Mr Heath, for long confused this issue by pretending that wages policy was necessary to combat inflation.[1] But

---

[1] Differential union monopoly and market power can alter relative prices, but not the general level of prices which is dominated by the money supply.

faced with a breakdown of the 5 per cent 'guideline', Mr Healey—that self-confessed 'unorthodox, neo-Keynesian monetarist'—is at last beginning to tell trade unions the truth, which is that the cost of irresponsible wage increases will be still higher unemployment.

Yet, despite the earlier political rhetoric about wages causing inflation, the Labour Government have all along conceded that wages had a direct connection with unemployment. Indeed, their boast that half-a-million jobs had been saved by a wage subsidy averaging £20 per worker gave the game away. It was implicitly an admission that trade unions were busily pricing their members out of work and then calling on taxpayers to undo part of the damage by bribing employers to keep uneconomic jobs going. The logical extension of this analysis at the margin confirms that present unemployment is higher than it would be if differential wages were free to find their market-clearing levels at rates which reflect the varying marginal productivity of labour—measured in goods and services that consumers are prepared to pay for.

Damaging effects of labour monopoly bargaining
Notwithstanding the pyrotechnics of latter-day Cambridge economists, this analysis of the damaging effects on employment of bargaining by labour monopolies cannot be dismissed as ideological prejudice. It is a finding of scientific analysis. It follows, in other words, from the way the real world works, and not the way we wish it worked. As that Cambridge giant of an earlier age, Professor (Sir) Dennis Robertson, wrote in 1930:[2]

'It does not need any remote calculations about the motives of savers to establish the proposition that an over-ambitious wage policy will cause unemployment.'

He concluded by drawing an inference—of which the cautionary latter half survives as germane to our discussion of practical policy almost half a century later:

'. . . there is more scope for improving the distribution of wealth along the lines of progressive taxation than along the lines of trade union pressure; though (short of Mr Dobb's revolution) there is not unlimited scope along either.'

For non-Cambridge economists, I should add that Mr Maurice Dobb was an old-fashioned Marxist and the author of the Cambridge

---

[2]Essay on 'Wage-Grumbles', in *Economic Fragments*, King, 1931.

Economic Handbook on *Wages*. Half a century later, we have had the revolution in wealth distribution (without Mr Dobb's assistance) through a devastating combination of inflation, progressive taxation and unindexed thresholds. So we are left with still more powerful trade unions which, having exhausted whatever limited scope there was for redistributing wealth in favour of their members, yet retain grotesquely enlarged powers to retard output, raise wages and so redistribute more of their members from employment into unemployment.

1 Does Job Creation Work?

JOHN T. ADDISON
University of Aberdeen

The Author

DR JOHN T. ADDISON: Born in 1946 and educated at Bournemouth School and the London School of Economics. Lecturer in Political Economy, University of Aberdeen, since 1972. Economic Adviser, Office of Manpower Economics, 1971-72; Visiting Professor of Economics, Temple University, 1975-76; and Visiting Assocate Professor of Economics, University of Guelph, 1979. Former economic consultant to National Board for Prices and Incomes, Commission on Industrial Relations and the OECD. Author of: (with W. S. Siebert) *The Market for Labor: An Analytical Treatment*, (Goodyear/Prentice-Hall, Santa Monica, California, 1979); (with J. Burton) *The Explanation of Inflation* (Macmillan, 1979—forthcoming); and *Wage Policies and Collective Bargaining Developments in Finland, Ireland and Norway* (OECD, Paris, 1979). Has contributed articles to *Applied Economics*, *British Journal of Industrial Relations*, *Research in Labor Economics*, *Scottish Journal of Political Economy*. For the IEA he contributed 'The Balance of Market Advantage', in *Trade Unions: Public Goods or Public 'Bads'?* (Readings 17, 1978).

I. INTRODUCTION

Major swings in economic activity are often paralleled by swings in fashion of economic policies. As the current recession has unfolded, and with it the emergence of stagflation, many countries have seen job creation as holding out the twin advantages of reducing unemployment while at the same time moderating the inflationary pressure at any given volume of unemployment. If such measures possess these attributes, they represent an uncovering rather than a discovery of the philosopher's stone. Arguably, that stone was first discovered some 40 years ago by Professor Kaldor,[1] and (perversely) buried during the sustained period of post-war boom.

I shall interpret 'job creation' literally and thus restrict my attention to an analysis of the creation of additional jobs,[2] by both indirect and direct methods.

II. JOB SUBSIDIES

Job subsidies are in part a reflex response to the perceived failure of orthodox Keynesian macro-economic analysis to provide a diagnosis of—still less a remedy for[3]—stagflation and slumpflation.[4] As confidence in Keynesian policies has waned, so governments have increasingly turned to job subsidisation as a means of promoting or

---

[1] N. Kaldor, 'Wage Subsidies as a Remedy for Unemployment', *Journal of Political Economy*, 1936, 44, pp. 721-742.

[2] This emphasis is at once convenient and appropriate. Job preserving subsidy schemes are widely acknowledged to offer the maximum potential for misuse and waste of public funds. First, the potential for fraud is maximised: the difficulty of screening applications for subsidies of this type creates an incentive for firms to overstate the magnitude of dismissals they are considering. Second, it is difficult to discriminate between applicants that will be viable enterprises in the long run, even if suffering temporarily from the recession, and those firms which are in permanent decline. Third, it is easy to see how political pressures can be brought to bear so as to ward off redundancies resulting from structural change. Job-preserving subsidies provide the classic example of fiscal illusion—where the benefits of government expenditure are clearly identified, but the costs are not—producing a structure of incentives which makes them likely to be adopted by political decision-takers.

[3] Abstracting from the neo-Keynesian emphasis upon incomes policy.

[4] The monetarist prescriptions are cold comfort when faced with an unemployment crisis due at least in some measure to past failure to accord with monetarist discipline.

maintaining employment. More positively, advocates of employment subsidies have claimed that these measures not merely cut unemployment but also simultaneously reduce the rate of price inflation and the size of the public sector borrowing requirement (PSBR).

Moreover, employment subsidies have also been advocated on the second-best ground that governments have traditionally subsidised capital rather than labour through investment grants and other devices, which has had the effect of biasing production methods away from labour.[5] Hence, subsidies to labour offer a means of rectifying a misallocation of resources created by previous policies. The issues raised by this second-best argument are important—analysis of the effects of investment and other grants to industry is a much neglected subject. The rationale of the approach is essentially that it takes a subsidy to kill a subsidy.[6] In my view, the economic theory of politics[7] has amply demonstrated the naivety of this general prescription.

Do job subsidies reduce the budget deficit?
Consider the effect of job subsidies on the PSBR. The claim that job subsidies can reduce the budget deficit rests upon the argument that the savings to the public purse from a reduction in unemployment exceed the expenditures on the subsidies.

First, there will be a reduction in transfer payments associated with the absorption of unemployed workers into employment and, second, the income and sales tax receipts of government will grow as workers transfer from unemployed to employed status. Santosh Mukherjee[8] has calculated that these exchequer savings amount to between 98 and 105 per cent of average male earnings in UK manu-

---

[5] B. Chiplin and P. J. Sloane, 'An Analysis of the Effectiveness of Manpower Policies and Related Measures in Curbing Unemployment in Britain and Sweden', Hamburg: Arbeitskreis Nr. 9, September 1978 (mimeographed).

[6] An intriguing American comparison of the relative effects of investment tax credits with equal cost blanket and marginal tax credits for employment is in J. R. Kesselman, S. H. Williams and E. R. Berndt, 'Tax Credits for Employment Rather Than Investment', *American Economic Review*, 1977, 67, pp. 339-349.

[7] G. Tullock, *The Vote Motive*, Hobart Paperback No. 9, IEA, 1976.

[8] S. Mukherjee, *The Costs of Unemployment*, Broadsheet No. 561, PEP, London, 1976.

facturing for a single man, and between 89 and 96 per cent for a married man with two children.[9] Somewhat more cautious estimates provided by the Manpower Services Commission suggest that, for a married man on average earnings with a 'non-working' wife and two children, the total financial costs to the government between the second and sixth month of unemployment exceed the amount the individual would have earned.[10] Mukherjee deduces from his data that subsidies of up to about 90 per cent of the average industrial wage would lead to a reduction of the budget deficit. A basic flaw in this reasoning is that it totally neglects the *certainty* of job losses (below, pp. 17-19) arising from the process of subsidisation. Equally important is its failure to consider the crucial factor of the time-dimension of job subsidisation relative to the time-dimension of unemployment.

Blanket employment subsidies, whereby employers are given a subsidy for every employee, cannot be expected to reduce the PSBR for the basic reason that the vast majority would be paid out for workers already in employment. Accordingly, there would be no 'saving on the dole'[11] accruing here. Marginal job subsidies, of the net accessions variety, could conceivably reduce the PSBR. In strictly micro-economic terms, the requirement is that the net accessions to expanding firms are met entirely from the stock of unemployed workers whose average duration of unemployment exceeds the average duration of subsidisation per job created. While it is misleading to regard unemployment simply as an aggregate, these restrictions are unlikely to be met in practice. Thus we can be reasonably certain that marginal subsidies will entail an increase in the PSBR. Macro-economic estimates provided by Drs Richard Layard and Steven Nickell suggest that a marginal job subsidy of one-third average industrial earnings would, on reasonable assumptions,

---

[9] Professor Rehn, working with data for Europe as a whole, calculates that the transference of a worker from the category of insured unemployment to income-earning employment typically results in exchequer savings that average 80 per cent of the wage. (G. Rehn, 'Recent Trends in Western Economics: Needs and Methods for Further Development of Manpower Policy', in E. Ginzberg *et al.*, *Re-examining European Manpower Policies*, National Commission for Manpower Policy, Washington, DC: US Government Printing Office, 1976, pp. 53-72.)

[10] Manpower Services Commission, *Review and Plan*, HMSO, London, 1977.

[11] To use the terminology of R. Kahn, 'The Relation of Home Investment to Unemployment', *Economic Journal*, 1931, 41, pp. 173-198.

entail an annual budget-deficit cost per job of between £1,100 and £2,500.[12] The advantages of job subsidies are apparently to be sought elsewhere.

Do job subsidies reduce inflation?
What then of the effects of employment subsidy measures on inflation? The 'dampening effect' of job subsidies on the rate of inflation is traditionally viewed as working through three main channels.

First, they are said to have a direct cost-reducing effect on the average labour costs of subsidised firms. As prices are related to costs, and labour costs are typically a large element in total costs, job subsidies might therefore lead to price reductions (below, p. 17).

Second, reductions in unit overhead costs are achieved by enabling firms beset by depression to work their plant closer to full capacity. Again, to the extent that the cost reduction feeds through into firms' prices, the rate of inflation could be dampened.

Third, there is the so-called indirect monetary effect, on the presumption that job subsidies reduce the budget deficit.[13]

If, for the reasons advanced above, the budget deficit prospect is unfavourable, what is the potential for reduced inflation offered by the potential reductions in average labour costs and unit overhead costs? The short answer is 'precious little'. Both arguments rest on a confusion between *levels* and *rates of change* of prices. As Mr John Burton has shown,[14] a job subsidy cannot permanently reduce the rate of inflation *via* these two effects unless the size of the subsidy is escalated in each successive period. Thus, a job subsidy fixed in nominal terms or as a proportion of the employee's wage will

---

[12]P. R. G. Layard and S. J. Nickell, *The Case for Subsidising Extra Jobs*, Discussion Paper No. 15 (revised), Centre for Labour Economics, London School of Economics, July 1978.

[13]Although there is no necessary direct connection between the rate of expansion of the money supply and the volume of public spending or the size of the budget deficit, it may plausibly be argued that, if job subsidies have the claimed effect on the budget deficit, they will to this extent reduce the pressure on the government to resort to money creation as a method of financing the deficit, and conversely.

[14]J. Burton, 'A Micro-Economic Analysis of Employment Subsidy Programmes', School of Economics and Politics, Kingston Polytechnic, 1977 (mimeographed).

achieve only a *temporary* reduction in the rate of increase in the costs and prices of subsidised firms during the period of its introduction. Thereafter, the rate of increase in costs experienced by such firms will resume its normal (that is, without subsidy) time-path. Both channels simply alter the timing of cost and price increases[15] over the duration of the subsidy programme. There will be no reduction in the average rate of inflation measured over the same period.

Do job subsidies reduce total unemployment?
That a job subsidy is capable of increasing or maintaining employment in firms/industries within its jurisdiction is not in doubt. The more fundamental question is whether job subsidies have a positive effect on unemployment *as a whole*. Marginal job subsidies offer more scope for increases in employment than do equal cost 'blanket' schemes where the subsidy is spread over all workers. The same revenue cost here can finance a larger percentage change in the price of subsidised units of labour and should therefore provide a stronger substitution towards employment of labour (so long as the firm accepts the marginal subsidy). But Layard and Nickell caution that *any* subsidy can have only a limited impact on *domestic* demand.[16] The principal effect is *via* prices, and prices cannot fall below the average costs of the marginal firm. Accordingly, since the responsiveness of aggregate demand to changes in price is low, the effect of any subsidy upon domestic demand is relatively small. Aggregate employment in an industry will rise only to the extent that average cost has fallen as a result of the marginal subsidy.[17]

A quite different situation may, however, rule in international markets. Layard and Nickell note that many firms are 'price-takers' in the usually competitive markets for internationally-traded goods, so that a large fall in the marginal cost of producing them will have a

---

[15]Assuming mark-up pricing and a constant trend rate of growth of labour productivity.

[16]Layard and Nickell, *op. cit.*

[17]Assume all firms in a competitive industry are in equilibrium. Now consider a marginal wage subsidy that results in a large expansion of industry supply. This will lead to a large fall in price within the industry and since average costs will have fallen only modestly, firms will be making losses. Industry output will subsequently contract until in equilibrium the price of output will be equal to the average cost in the marginal firm.

large effect on the quantity sold, even if there is only a small fall in their average costs.

Distortion of labour costs structure

Yet marginal subsidies inevitably alter the structure of labour costs in the economy. They reduce the relative costs of firms receiving the subsidies and raise the relative costs of non-subsidised firms. Thus, marginal employment subsidies give rise to a *displacement effect:* the stimulation of employment in subsidised firms occurs at the cost of jobs lost in non-subsidised firms. Such effects are not necessarily immediate, which compounds the difficulty of establishing the true net effects of marginal subsidies. Rather unsatisfactory official estimates suggest a displacement effect which may eventually approach between one-third and one-half of the jobs provided under the (job preserving) Temporary Employment Subsidy.[18]

To the extent that advocates of job subsidies do recognise a covert loss of jobs, they would also point to the offsetting demand 'multiplier' effects of subsidies as clinching the argument in their favour. However, as Burton reminds us,[19] the simple multiplier theorems of Keynesian economic analysis hold only if (a) the change in conditions of demand initiated by the authorities does not alter the expectations and behaviour of non-government participants, and (b) the potential side-effects of deficit financing on output and employment can be ignored.

Both assumptions have come under strong challenge. Thus, it is now widely accepted that workers, firms and households form expectations about their economic environment, including government behaviour, and adapt their own behaviour accordingly. This result has ramifications wider than the basic argument that a *permanent* increase in the rate of inflation cannot sustain more than a *temporary* fall in unemployment (below, pp. 18-19). Moreover, both forms of deficit finance—money creation or the issue of debt—are capable of 'crowding out' output and employment equivalent to that

---

[18]An interesting and rather different interpretation of the displacement effects arising from direct job creation in the US public sector is given by M. Wiseman, 'Public Employment as Fiscal Policy', *Brookings Papers on Economic Activity*, 1976, 1, pp. 67-104.

[19]*The Job Support Machine: A Critique of the Subsidy Morass*, Centre for Policy Studies, London, 1979.

arising from the additional government expenditure through their effects on the rate of inflation and interest rates.[20]

But an important qualification to this latter argument, deriving from Layard/Nickell, is that marginal job subsidies give rise to a multiplier effect not primarily through the components of domestic demand but rather through the stimulation of exports. Job subsidies on this view are an explicit export subsidy. Assuming plausible cost and other assumptions, Layard/Nickell calculate that a marginal recruitment subsidy of one-third average industrial earnings would generate an increase in employment of between 0.7 and 1.0 per cent and improve the balance of payments by between 0.2 and 0.3 per cent of gross national product (GNP). Their analysis is persuasive. The reduction in unemployment, however, is achieved by simply exporting it, resulting in an *international* job displacement effect. It is a covert beggar-thy-neighbour policy and invites retaliation.

Further limitations of job subsidies
The limitations of job subsidies focus on the crucial question of their duration.

First, job subsidies might become a fossilised feature of the fiscal scene. That this danger is real may be illustrated by analysing the recovery phase of an economy moving out of recession. A decision to remove subsidies at some point in the recovery phase will always be seen to damage employment prospects in some firms/industries because of the uneven pattern of recovery across the economy. The lobbying pressure of laggers might well induce the authorities to postpone the winding-down of the programme, which could itself retard the achievement of full employment. More fundamentally, such pressures could result in a long-term programme of support. Indeed, the political incentive towards continued subsidisation is very strong and is reinforced by other factors such as the fiscal illusion of the tax-paying community.

Second, an amplification of the argument that, once the authorities start to spend extensively and predictably on job subsidies, workers and firms will begin to formulate expectations that undermine the effectiveness of the measures: the more unions become conditioned by government behaviour to expect the widespread implementation

---

[20]M. M. Carlson and R. W. Spencer, 'Crowding Out and Its Critics', *Federal Reserve Bank of St. Louis Review*, 1975, 57, pp. 2-17.

of subsidy programmes in recession, the stronger will be their resistance to cuts in real wages at such times and the more stubborn their intransigence in normal times.[21] The profound irony of this result is that Professor Kaldor originally argued that subsidies were the ideal form of policy instrument for unemployment generated by union-imposed wage rigidities!

Equally, this expectations-oriented reasoning can be applied to what economists term 'quasi-contract' labour markets. The notion of the quasi-contract was introduced to explain the existence of lay-offs and pro-cyclical quit behaviour,[22] neither of which phenomena is at first blush satisfactorily tackled by modern neo-classical search theories.[23] Assume, first, that workers are more risk averse than firms and, second, that implicit contracts exist which cause firms and workers to act as if they are legally constrained. If the first assumption is correct, it will be mutually advantageous *a priori* for the firm to offer workers a joint product consisting of employment and insurance against income instability. Thus, implicit contracts are formed. However, *ex ante*, one party may do better by breaking the contract. Firms are assumed to adhere to contracts because a reputation as a 'good employer' will, in the long run, reduce their wage bill. (It is less clear why workers should adhere to an unwritten contract, although subsequent research has confirmed the importance of mobility costs arising from firm-specific training.) The upshot of this new theory is that the higher the degree of job security provided and financed by government through employment subsidies in recession, the smaller is the incentive of employers to provide for job security through implicit agreements of this nature. Thus, in the long run, use of job subsidies as a continuous feature of counter-cyclical policy

---

[21]J. Burton, 'Depression Unemployment, Union Wage Rigidity and Employment Subsidies', *International Journal of Social Economics*, 1977, 4, pp. 48-54.

[22]That is, voluntary separations which rise in the upturn and fall in the downturn.

[23]The notion of the quasi-contract lies at the heart of a branch of micro-economic analysis that has become known as the 'new new' micro-economics. Key articles are C. Azariadis, 'Implicit Contracts and Underemployment Equilibria', *Journal of Political Economy*, 1975, 83, pp. 1,183-1,202; M. N. Baily, 'Wages and Employment Under Uncertain Demand', *Review of Economic Studies*, 1974, 41, pp. 37-50; D. F. Gordon, 'A Neo-classical Theory of Keynesian Unemployment', *Economic Inquiry*, 1974, 12, pp. 431-459.

could lead to the reshaping of quasi-contracts so as to raise the natural rate of unemployment towards which the system will tend in equilibrium.

III. PUBLIC SECTOR JOB CREATION

The case for direct job creation within the government economy rests on the same sort of arguments as in the analysis of job subsidies. For both sets of policy the assumption is that, on balance, fiscal policy 'works' in the sense that deficit-financed outlays can increase GNP and employment. Job creation within the public sector is favoured by those policy-makers who see in the very directness of the measures the prospect of 'a bigger bang per buck'.[24] Direct job creation is also the preferred policy instrument of those of 'dualist persuasion' (IV) and in general of those who see public service programmes as distributive and allocative policies offering improved equity in the distribution of income and jobs.

It follows that the objections raised in the discussion of blanket and marginal subsidies continue to apply to government job creation. American experience suggests further observations.[25] First, most job-creation measures of this type have amounted to almost pure movement along the Phillips curve[26] rather than shifting it. This kind of increase in the demand for labour is probably just as inflationary as any other, and would put the economy at a point of (temporary) lower unemployment and higher inflation that could be achieved by more traditional demand-stimulating measures. In practice, then, although lip service has been paid to the principle of selectivity— which offers some potential for lowering unemployment at a given rate of inflation (IV)—direct job creation has at best generated less

---

[24]An American term expressing the magnitude of the employment effect per budget dollar.

[25]For example, the references cited in Wiseman, *op. cit.;* D. Werneke, 'Job Creation Programs: The United States Experience', *International Labour Review*, 1976, 114, pp. 43-59; R. E. Hall, 'Prospects for Shifting the Phillips Curve through Manpower Policy', *Brookings Papers on Economic Activity*, 1971, 3, pp. 659-701.

[26]The Phillips curve in its simplest guise is an empirical relationship between wage (and price) inflation and excess demand. The latter variable is conventionally measured by the level of unemployment. The relationship is such that a fall in unemployment, resulting from an expansion of aggregate demand, is secured only at the cost of higher inflation.

21

inflation per point of reduction in the rate of unemployment than might have resulted through a general stimulation of demand *via* monetary and fiscal measures.

Second, the productivity of the jobs to be provided within the government sector: scepticism is heightened by their limited duration and the rather high-skill job requirements of many parts of the public sector contrasted with the skills possessed by unemployed workers in general. Only a small percentage of American 'public-service' job-holders appear to have been receiving unemployment insurance at the time of starting the programme, which points either to a high displacement of private sector jobs or poor implementation.

Third, as an employer of last resort, government is unlikely to fire workers who do not produce; this objection is heightened by the difficulty of evaluating the output of many government sector agencies. As a general rule, although some managers in the public sector will have an incentive to produce efficiently, even here more factor inputs (workers) will be employed than are required on profit-maximising grounds.[27]

On the assumption that idle capital in recession is concentrated in the private sector, one can therefore perhaps see the broad appeal of measures biased toward job creation in the private sector whereby capital as well as labour would be put to work.

IV. A CASE FOR JOB SUBSIDIES?

Is there a case for intervention on behalf of 'disadvantaged' workers? I shall consider the potential offered by selective job-creation measures to 'cheat' the Phillips curve.

A useful starting point is provided by the 'dual labour market' thesis.[28] The duality is between two sectors: a *primary* sector, offering 'good' jobs with high wages, satisfactory working conditions, security, and prospects for promotion; and a *secondary* sector, offering 'bad' jobs with poor wages and working conditions,

[27]W. A. Niskanen, *Bureaucracy: Servant or Master?*, Hobart Paperback No. 5, IEA, 1973.

[28]On the evolution of dual labour market theory, see D. M. Gordon, *Theories of Poverty and Unemployment*, Heath, Lexington, Mass., 1972, Chapter 4; G. G. Cain, 'The Challenge of Segmented Labor Market Theories to Orthodox Theory: A Survey', *Journal of Economic Literature*, 1976, 14, pp. 1,215-1,257.

frequent lay-offs, and little hope of advancement. A favoured portion of the labour force, particularly white adult males, enjoys the benefits of employment within the primary sector, while the rest (women, teenagers, and minorities) are trapped within the secondary market, where, in particular, there is high turnover and, usually, high unemployment. The problem, as viewed by the dualists, is not a shortage of jobs, even in recession, but a shortage of 'good' jobs.

Labour market duality—objections and qualifications
In analysing the primary sector, dualists have concentrated on describing the 'internal labour market'. Efficiency is said to play only a small part in its functioning; wage rates and jobs are distributed among primary workers according to factors such as custom rather than productivity. Moreover, the number of primary or skilled jobs is supposed to be unresponsive to the relative availability of skilled workers, so that expansion of human capital is unlikely to lead to an upgrading of the job structure. Indeed, dualists argue that large numbers of workers in the secondary sector *already* possess the human capital they need and can be trained for skilled jobs at no more than the usual cost. Their policy prescription is therefore the provision of more good jobs—a recommendation at odds with the neo-classical teaching that factors which improve the stock of human capital enhance the probability of success in finding jobs.

This analysis is open to a number of objections. If good workers are available, why do not new firms enter the market to exploit this reservoir—at least in the 'grey' areas intermediate between good and bad jobs where the barriers to entry erected by oligopolies and unions are less important? Three basic explanations have been offered for this lack of competitive response: overt discrimination, feedback, and statistical discrimination. Overt market discrimination refers to the exclusion (or underpayment) of qualified blacks *inter al.*, partly because of the prejudices of employers and, more important, fellow employees.[29] But an important contribution of the dualist analysis has been the emphasis placed on 'feedback' effects, where being trapped

---

[29] J. T. Addison and W. S. Siebert, *The Market for Labor: An Analytical Treatment*, Goodyear/Prentice-Hall, Santa Monica, Calif., 1979, Chapter 6.

in the secondary sector causes workers to adopt habits of work that are unsuitable for primary jobs: unstable attendance, poor work commitment, high turnover. Thus, unstable employment encourages workers who hold 'bad' jobs to become bad workers or, more precisely, to adopt 'bad' (i.e. inefficient) work habits. One obvious, although neglected, implication of the feedback effect is that, once the worker in the secondary sector has developed bad habits he is thereby less skilled and transferable than the primary worker, and, unlike the victim of discrimination, he is not under-employed.

'Statistical discrimination'—an information externality—arises where employers have difficulty in identifying productive workers. In this situation, employers may rely on characteristics such as age and skin colour, which are correlated with productivity, as an inexpensive screening mechanism. Thus an exceptional black worker, for example, has difficulty in getting a good job partly because employers will not be able to identify him as exceptional and will assume that he is closer to the average of all blacks than he is. Where information is hard to get, this kind of behaviour on the part of the employer is perfectly rational. The real issue here is an empirical one: how pervasive are these informational externalities? Undoubtedly, full employment induces employers to experiment and revise their notions of stereotype groups.

Neither feedback nor information externalities can sustain labour market duality. What of the overt discrimination explanation? It is a moot point whether minority groups are seriously disadvantaged in labour markets *given their endowments.* This is not to deny that current endowments reflect past discrimination in education funding or that those who believe they will receive a lower return from their training will undertake less training; but there is little firm evidence to suggest the presence of pervasive secondary under-employment.

Nevertheless, I would argue that good jobs are scarce relative to a socially optimal supply. But this inefficiency results from factors long recognised in neo-classical economics and not from the dualist type of inefficiencies. Market power, for example, results in a socially inefficient under-supply of good jobs. High wages that are not offset by savings in the form of reduced labour turnover restrict the output of the primary sector (and hence the derived demand for good jobs) and generate a substitution towards capital and away from skilled labour. Also, imperfections inherent in the labour market result in an under-investment in specific training.[30] Because workers cannot sign voluntary indenture contracts, investment in specific capital is necessarily more risky than investment in physical capital. The result is a discrepancy between private and social returns to specific training. Under-investment in specific training by firms and workers is a 'social' problem that requires remedial action.

This conclusion does not imply that the internal labour market operates without regard to efficiency. Indeed, it has been cogently argued that the structured internal labour market is best viewed as an *efficient institutional response* by firms to the basic market imperfections arising from the costs of information and of specific and on-the-job training. Even an efficient internal labour market will not solve externality problems, and the number of 'good' jobs will tend to be less than a social optimum.[31]

Secondary labour market and job training
While there is little concrete evidence of pervasive secondary underemployment,[32] the dualist analysis gives a good description of the functioning of the lowest-wage sector. To this extent, it complements the traditional neo-classical analysis of 'segmentation' which recognises the barriers to mobility caused by unequal endowments of human capital. Secondary workers have a tenuous attachment to particular jobs and to work in general. Low wages, job instability and frequent *short* spells of unemployment are the ingredients of the problem for policy caused by the working poor. The broad social costs of high turnover and the external effects of specific training make a case for encouraging firms to reduce turnover and to undertake specific and on-the-job training. As for unemployment among the poor or 'problem' groups, the social opportunity costs depend very much on the suggested alternative. If judged by the available un-

---

[30]G. S. Becker, *Human Capital*, National Bureau of Economic Research, New York, 2nd Edition, 1975, p. 32.

[31]The efficiency argument is presented by O. E. Williamson, M. L. Wachter and J. E. Harris, 'Understanding the Employment Relation: The Analysis of Idiosyncratic Exchange', *Bell Journal of Economics*, 1975, 6, pp. 250-278.

[32]In the sense that its workers are potentially skilled enough to function in the primary sector *given the usual training costs*, but are prevented by discrimination, imperfect information and the failure of primary sector firms to adjust their job structure to employ available good workers. The feed-back effect only reinforces this conclusion.

skilled jobs that require no training, the cost is relatively low. But if employment with useful on-the-job training is a feasible alternative, the cost of, say, youth unemployment is substantially higher than the immediate loss in output.

In general, it can be argued that more good jobs will emerge in response to an increased supply of skilled workers. Hence there is a case for programmes of manpower training and new subsidies (or taxes) designed to encourage the private sector to expand on-the-job training. These measures will be difficult to administer and slow to work, most obviously because they require the adoption of new production techniques. Neither institutional nor on-the-job training will achieve their ultimate goal in big leaps; secondary workers will only be upgraded a step at a time. As Professor Robert E. Hall of MIT has shown, the success of individual programmes will depend crucially on how well they are constructed and funded.[33] Dramatic effects on unemployment are thus ruled out.

Economic growth and capital accumulation, associated with periods of *stable* and high demand, emerge as the most crucial ingredients in providing more good jobs. Moreover, to the extent that the high unemployment rates of 'disadvantaged' workers are not an equilibrium phenomenon, which means that problem groups vary in their excess supply, more dramatic effects on unemployment can be achieved by reversing past measures that have prevented relative wages from adjusting themselves, thereby throwing the adjustment process on to unemployment rates. Here I am referring to such factors as the extension of minimum wage legislation and changes in unemployment compensation/welfare benefits. Also, there is the vexed question of the job regulatory practices of trade unions, where the requirement seems to be compensation for their abandonment.[34]

Selective public sector job provision for 'disadvantaged' groups?
An appreciation of the issues involved in improving the lot of 'disadvantaged' workers can be obtained from a recent study by Baily and Tobin.[35] Although the measures they investigated do not

---

[33]Hall, *op. cit.*

[34]Addison and Siebert, *op. cit.*, Chapter 9.

[35]M. N. Baily and J. Tobin, 'Macroeconomic Effects of Selective Public Employment and Wage Subsidies', *Brookings Papers on Economic Activity*, 1977, 2, pp. 511-541.

correspond to those proposed above because of their much more sweeping nature, they graphically indicate the costs and benefits of attempts to alter the mix of employment in favour of workers who, in the normal course of events, experience high rates of unemployment. The basic proposal is that governments should directly hire (or subsidise other employers to hire) workers whose unemployment does little or nothing to restrain the advance of wage costs in the aggregate. For this strategy to be successful, 'selective eligibility' is essential.[36] Open-ended employer-of-last-resort programmes (III) and general employment subsidies would fail to cheat the Phillips curve, i.e. achieve higher rates of employment with lower inflation.

Baily and Tobin Mark I
Baily and Tobin work with two basic models. The first identifies the ways in which direct job creation might reduce the volume of frictional unemployment—that unemployment which accompanies the process of matching workers and jobs. The scope for this effect arises from holding wages in the programme *below* market levels, coupled with restricting jobs to an eligible group lacking good opportunities elsewhere. Wage inflation is related directly to vacancies and inversely to unemployment. Normally, when additional jobs are created, vacancies also increase; hence it takes more newly-created jobs (or job slots) to produce a net increase in actual employment (or filled jobs).

Direct job creation in the public sector could improve the trade-off between inflation and unemployment (the Phillips curve) and the minimal non-accelerating inflation rate of unemployment by reducing frictional unemployment. *First*, it may diminish the extra vacancies that accompany additional jobs, because the creation of additional job vacancies resulting from direct job creation should be minimal. *Second*, it might be associated with a particularly small induced labour-supply effect because of its selectivity, transient

---

[36]'Selective eligibility' means that the programme must be *targeted* towards specific groups on the basis of such criteria as low income, welfare dependency, previous unemployment, residence in a labour surplus area, youth, and so on.

nature, and low wage content. *Third*, the programme might reduce the wage pressure associated with a given state of the labour market. To have this effect, however, it must not reduce the incentive to look for alternatives. The programme should provide a channel for routing unemployed workers to vacancies in the private sector; i.e., they should continue to look for and be available for other jobs much as they would if they were ordinarily unemployed. Again, this effect would be facilitated by holding down wage rates, limiting the frequency of such programmes and encouraging placement in the private sector. In the light of the earlier discussion, however, it is clear that transient jobs of this nature are unlikely to build up human capital or encourage careers. The proposal also appears to be based on an uncritical assumption of involuntary unemployment. There is also the standard difficulty that direct job-creation measures of this kind gloss over the motivations of politicians and bureaucrats.

Baily and Tobin Mark II

The authors' second model deals more substantively with a segmented labour market comprising imperfectly substitutable adult and teenager groups. In this approach, the power of selective employment policies comes from exploiting differences between the two labour markets in response to changes in wages. The details of the model are in the Appendix, but the basic argument is as follows. Government programmes that hire additional teenagers will lower their supply to private employers, thus raising the wages of teenagers relatively to adults. This in turn displaces some teenagers in private employment but, because of the substitutability assumption, they are only partially displaced and a net reduction in unemployment is achieved.

Baily and Tobin show that such programmes can raise real GNP as well as reducing the number of persons unemployed—unless the Phillips curve for teenagers is considerably steeper than that for adults at a given level of demand. The main thrust of the argument is that direct job creation shifts the burden of unemployment from one group (teenagers) to another (adults). If teenagers have a sufficiently flat Phillips curve, then the total unemployment rate consistent with non-accelerating inflation can be lowered by shifting employment towards them but only at the cost of higher adult unemployment.

Baily and Tobin suggest that direct job creation (or employment subsidies[37]) is likely to reduce unemployment significantly. The virtue of their analysis, emphasising as it does that gains in GNP are harder to come by than crude reductions in unemployment, is that it makes explicit the costs of attempting to reduce unemployment among disadvantaged groups.

V. CONCLUSIONS

A review of the cases for and against marginal and blanket job subsidies leads to a sceptical and pessimistic conclusion. The claims of the proponents of such measures appear on close inspection to be largely false. A similar conclusion holds for direct job creation of the open-ended, 'employer-of-last-resort' variety. Nevertheless, I have presented a case for a margin of *selective* or *targeted* job subsidisation on the grounds of external effects inherent in specific training and the social costs of high labour turnover. But the effects of these selective measures are by their very nature unlikely to be pronounced, and major inroads into unemployment must be sought elsewhere. My own prejudice is towards a market solution, for economic growth and capital accumulation associated with periods of high and stable demand are the most important ingredients in providing more and better jobs.

It is arguable that a restoration of profits from their present low levels (in real terms) is a cheaper, more efficient method of reducing unemployment than either subsidies or direct job creation.[38] But the main task of this paper has been not to analyse the market solution but rather to elaborate the issues involved in direct and indirect job creation. Job subsidies, in my view, do not change the fundamental forces determining the rate of wage inflation, which provide the key to the solution. They must therefore be regarded as peripheral instruments.

---

[37]They argue that the possibilities of reducing the non-accelerating inflation rate of unemployment through selective wage subsidies depend on essentially the same circumstances that make job creation effective. Their results suggest that wage subsidies are in general less effective than direct job-creation measures per budget dollar. But the issue of 'bang per buck' is only one consideration in a comparative evaluation of the two types of measure. I would argue that selective job subsidies, possibly operated by a voucher scheme, are the more promising instrument.

[38]This argument is amplified by R. Morley, 'Unemployment, Profits' Share and Regional Policy', in A. Whiting (ed.), *The Economics of Industrial Subsidies*, HMSO, London, 1976, pp. 159-182.

APPENDIX
The Baily-Tobin Segmented Labour Market Model
Consider a segmented labour market in which adults (group 1) and teen-agers (group 2) are imperfect substitutes at prevailing wages. Two sectoral wage-change equations can be specified:

$$\overset{1}{\dot{W}_1} = f(\alpha_1 U_1, \alpha_2 U_2 - 1nR) + \text{expectational terms},$$

$$\overset{1}{f_1} < \overset{1}{f_2} < 0, \overset{1}{f_3} > 0;$$

$$\overset{2}{\dot{W}_2} = f(\alpha_1 U_1, \alpha_2 U_2, 1nR) + \text{expectational terms},$$

$$\overset{2}{f_2} < \overset{2}{f_1} < 0, \overset{2}{f_3} > 0.$$

Both unemployment rates appear in each equation. The two types of worker are in some degree substitutes, and unemployment of each type restrains both wage-rates. But the derivatives show that each wage-rate is more sensitive to unemployment of the type of labour in that market. The unemployment rates, U_1 and U_2, are weighted by shares in the labour force, α_1 and α_2; and the ratio of the levels of the two wage-rates, W_1/W_2, is given by R. In this comparative context, the assumption is that each sectoral wage rises faster, other things equal, when that sector's wage is low relative to the other. The feedback terms are such that an equal increase in the two expected rates of wage inflation will raise both actual rates of wage increase equally.

Type 1 unemployment falls with R. When the relative wage is high, type 1 workers will moderate their wage demands, recognising the potential for substituting secondary workers. Thus, a high W_1 relative to W_2 dampens the pressure for wage increases and helps to reduce the rate of unemployment. Similarly, type 2 unemployment rises with R—for a given $\dot{W}_2$ the required U_2 is higher when R is higher.

Effect of relative wage criterion
Had the relative wage been omitted from the equations it would be seen that direct job creation is pointless in the long run. The two equations $f^1 = 0, f^2 = 0$ (the required condition for a minimal non-accelerating inflation rate of unemployment) would now determine *unique* values of each unemployment rate $(\alpha_1 U_1, \alpha_2 U_2)$ at which $\dot{W}_1 = \dot{W}_2 = \dot{W}e_1 = \dot{W}e_2$, where $\dot{W}e_1$ and $\dot{W}e_2$ are the expectational or feedback terms. Thus, if teenagers were hired in public sector jobs, their unemployment rates would fall which would lead to a bidding-up of their relative wage and a substitution of adults for teenagers in private unemployment. Assuming that macro-policy was directed to countering wage acceleration, this process would end

when a number of teenagers equal to the number inducted into public sector jobs had been displaced from private employment.

But with R included in the equations, there *is* scope for reducing teenage unemployment—admittedly at the cost of increasing adult unemployment—consistent with the maintenance of a minimal non-accelerating inflation rate of unemployment. Specifically, the two equations $f^1 = 0, f^2 = 0$ determine $\alpha_1 U_1$ and $\alpha_2 U_2$, each as a function of R:

$$\alpha_1 U_1 = S^1(R), \quad S^1_R < 0;$$
$$\alpha_2 U_2 = S^2(R), \quad S^2_R > 0.$$

There is thus a locus of employment combination $(\alpha_1 LU_1, \alpha_2 LU_2)$, where L is the labour force) that meet $f^1 = f^2 = 0$. The slope of this locus $[\delta(\alpha_2 U_2)]/[\delta(\alpha_1 U_1)]$ is S^2_R/S^1_R. Movement up the locus is associated with increases in R, and hence increases in teenage unemployment and decreases in adult unemployment.

The steeper the locus is at the point the economy reaches in the absence of a job-creation policy, the larger is the potential reduction in aggregate unemployment from policies varying U_1 and U_2 along the locus. All that is necessary to reduce aggregate unemployment $(L_1 U_1 + L_2 U_2)$ is that the slope of the locus exceed -1, where the latter denotes the slope of a line recording points of equal count. Indeed, if the slope of the locus is steeper than the relative wage it is also possible to reduce wage-weighted unemployment and, therefore, GNP on the assumption that relative wages match relative marginal products.[1]

Other effects of relative wage change on labour demand

However, it is also necessary to take account of the exogenous or induced effects on labour demand resulting from the adjustment of relative wages. The decline in R will cause a substitution of adult workers for teenage workers in private production, thereby diminishing the effectiveness of direct job creation. This effect will be more pronounced the more perfect are the substitution possibilities. Thus, if the two types of worker are perfect substitutes for each other, and the observed relative wage indicates the constant rate of substitution in initial equilibrium, direct job creation will be fruitless. Here, an equal number of teenagers will be displaced from

---

[1] Baily and Tobin demonstrate that, under reasonable assumptions, the slope of the locus is likely to be steeper than the relative wage. Using 1974 sectoral unemployment values, it emerges that the slope of the teenage-worker Phillips curve would have to be greater than 14 times that of the corresponding adult curve at a given level of unemployment in each sector before a lowering of U_2 (with its inflationary effect just neutralised by a rise of U_1) would fail to increase GNP as well as cutting aggregate unemployment.

the private sector. If, on the other hand, the two types of worker are imperfect substitutes—as is indeed likely—the private employment of both groups will be lower than under initial equilibrium, although aggregate unemployment will fall.

On the basis of a formal analysis of substitution, Baily and Tobin provide rough quantitative pointers as to the effect of direct job creation for teenagers upon teenage/aggregate unemployment and for GNP different parameter values of the elasticity of substitution, locus slope and responsiveness of unemployment to relative wages in the adult sector. The positive effect on teenage/aggregate unemployment is seen to be larger, the lower the elasticity of substitution, the steeper the locus slope and the higher the unemployment responsiveness of the adult sector. Gains in GNP emerge as harder to achieve than reductions in aggregate unemployment.

Questions and Discussion

JOHN B. WOOD (*Institute of Economic Affairs*): Does Dr Addison regard the dual labour-market concept, which I must confess I have not heard of before, as useful or not? He introduced it at one stage but, as he was making the distinction, it occurred to me that the whole thing was perfectly explicable in other ways. The concept is explicable within the normal terms of the different productivities of teenagers, women, blacks, and so on. And insofar as that does not explain the phenomenon, it could be explained in terms of the restraints by way of the legal framework or custom in the proper working of the labour market. And then I thought at a later stage you yourself referred to productivity as being largely the explanation. Is it a useful concept? Is it illuminating or not?

DR ADDISON: I used the dual labour-market hypothesis simply to locate my subsequent argument in favour of a margin of selective job subsidisation. You will recall my contention that there is indeed likely to be a shortage of good jobs in the so-called primary sector arising from the costs of information and of specific and on-the-job training, though *not* from the dualist type of inefficiencies. Having said this, the dualists have added to our understanding, although only in a descriptive sense, of the workings of the lowest wage sectors of the economy. From this we can test, for example, whether the disadvantage of those finding employment in the secondary sector is of a continuing or temporary nature. Moreover, the dualists have made an important contribution in bringing to the attention of neo-classical economists the role of feedback effects, whereby location if not entrapment in the secondary sector causes workers to acquire habits of work that are inappropriate for primary jobs, and that are difficult to shed when they are offered good jobs—a not unimportant consideration, I submit, and one with obvious cost implications for programmes seeking to upgrade job skills.

In short, I found the dual labour-market hypothesis to be a useful peg on which to hang my own particular line of argument that there is likely to be a shortage of good jobs within the primary sector. It was also worthwhile examining the various dualist arguments in their own right given the topic before this Seminar. Dual labour-market analysts do after all have their own distinctive set of policy proposals for dealing with unemployment, namely direct job creation—and their arguments require a sensible airing rather than outright dismissal.

RALPH HARRIS (*Chairman*): I would have thought a bridge might be constructed between Mr Wood and our speaker. If you take account of social and political factors which impose some floor to the labour market— in an implicit minimum wage effect—I interpreted part of what Dr Addison had to say as being to improve the employability of those whose wages had been raised by such 'distortions' above the value of their contribution to output.

CHRISTOPHER MEAKIN (*then Director for Smaller Firms, CBI*): Dr Addison's introduction spelt out very well the sort of job subsidies we are talking about. It is generally known that the small firms sector in this country has been singled out to be the recipients of most of this sort of subsidy. So I thought I would offer a couple of anecdotes, which the academics among us can analyse and dissect at leisure. Listening to a very good cross-section of small firms from all over the UK, including the most favoured areas for subsidies of all kinds like Northern Ireland or Scotland, the reception given to the latest announcement of goodies to be handed out to small firms is an absolutely deafening silence. And if you push the Small Firms Council of the CBI hard enough, and ask them for an opinion on these latest subsidies, you eventually get a faint booing noise. But it takes a long time to get a reaction. They are highly sceptical of the input costs, if I can borrow an economist's term to use in a non-economic sense, that is, of raising the resources that are eventually doled out by the bureaucratic system to the small business community. There is a strong suspicion that, somewhere in between the money going into the bureaucratic system through one form of taxation or another and coming out again, something like a 30 per cent reduction takes place for overheads, or perhaps more.

The sort of noises that are made among small firms, in committees and councils, and also in the letters that cross my desk, are very critical. One criticism is about the size of company. The sort of new job subsidies we are talking about are only handed out to companies on the rather artificial and often frustrating criterion of 200 employees or less. This immediately generates two difficulties. One is that the company at present getting job subsidies and with, say, 199 workers is wondering exactly what to do next. Does it grow and wipe out the whole lot, or does it stop growing? Then there is a competitive problem, in the form of a scream from the company up the road or in the same market elsewhere, that says: 'Our closest competitor, because it is just a bit smaller than we are, is getting all sorts of lovely job subsidies and either stealing our business, if it is in the same market, or stealing our workers, if it is in the same geographical area'.

A further problem that seems to arise is the inevitable wish of those drafting the principles of subsidy to single out this or that for favoured treatment. The latest gimmick is the, again, rather artificial distinction between industrial and non-industrial employment. The idea is that there is something better and more beneficial in subsidising industrial employment, presumably on the grounds that people get their hands dirty doing it.

These are the sort of problems that these job subsidy policies provoke among small firms—I am not even venturing into the much more vexed territory of the very big firm *versus* the small firm.

PROF. ALBERT REES (*Princeton University*): It may be unfair for one speaker to participate in the discussion of another speaker's paper, but the subject of this paper is rather different from mine and Dr Addison did refer to American experience with direct job-creation programmes. In particular he referred to a paper by Bailey and Tobin; I have just been reading the volume in which that paper appears, called *Creating Jobs*, edited by John Palmer for the Brookings Institution. Reading these papers leads me to a view of American job-creation programmes on which I want to ask for Dr Addison's comments.

If one views the job-creation programme as an alternative to creating jobs in the private sector simply by the process of increasing aggregate demand, the alleged advantage of the job-creation programme is that it is targeted on the 'disadvantaged' groups. And there I would say American experience is fairly discouraging, and that job-creation in the government or non-profit sector shows that the targeting does not seem to work very well. The people who get these jobs do not have secondary labour-market characteristics, they have the characteristics more of workers in the primary labour market. There is also a strong presumption, at least for someone who believes in the free market, that the output created by the public sector jobs is less valuable than the output that would be created in private sector jobs. This therefore looks like a second-best solution.

Having said that, though, it is possible that there is a different standard of comparison, that jobs in the public sector created under a job-creation programme are really not an alternative to jobs in the private sector but an alternative to transfer payments (i.e. unemployment and other social benefits). And the paper that brings this out most clearly is by Jonathan Kesselman of the University of British Columbia, which reviews the big job-creation programme in the Great Depression, when it was felt strongly that what you were choosing between was not public jobs *versus* private jobs but public jobs *versus* the dole. It was thought desirable that people should do some work in return for transfer payments and not simply have transfer payments handed out to them. If that is the choice in practice, then it may well be that job creation reduces public spending because the supply of people who are lining up for the dole, for transfer payments, for income maintenance payments of whatever kind, may be smaller if you impose a work requirement, even if the work being done is not terribly useful (and some is not). Looking at that comparison, do you see a possibility of a job-creation programme being deficit-reducing, or reducing what you call the public sector borrowing requirement?

DR ADDISON: The short answer to Professor Rees is that I do not know whether the imposition of some form of work requirement would be deficit-reducing. Clearly, it might deter some and, in particular, potential labour-market entrants. But it is a rather unusual interpretation he offers. Anyway, I would judge the work requirement stipulation to be politically infeasible in a British context. More broadly, I have little faith in direct job-creation measures and would strongly endorse Professor Rees's pessimism as regards the US experience while resisting his particular standard of comparison. All the studies with which I am familiar point to such jobs being taken by those who are not unemployed or by those who would have found employment without difficulty. In other words, US programme entrants have proved more employable than even the average unemployed worker. Again, I do not see direct job creation as the answer.

I have instead presented a case for a margin of subsidisation to encourage firms to undertake specific and on-the-job training, to reduce turnover for reasons associated with the external effects inherent in specific training and the social costs of turnover. I also favour conventional manpower measures of the re-training variety because the labour market will respond to changes in relevant factors and availabilities. In neither case, however, are dramatic inroads into the unemployment count to be expected—the programmes in question being difficult to administer and slow to work. Yet I see such measures as preferable to the superficial quick solution offered by direct job creation.

I have interpreted the high unemployment experience of disadvantaged groups as an equilibrium phenomenon. To the extent that this is not the case, fairly substantial reductions in unemployment might be obtained by tackling those rigidities that have thrown the adjustment processes on to quantities. Perhaps in this latter context I might have paid more attention to unemployment as a constraint on choice in the first instance rather than the result of choice. However, I did not seek to get overly involved in the voluntary/involuntary debate because the mere presence of involuntary unemployment does not of itself imply a compelling rationale for any government to intervene or to compensate it, because private markets may already have done so. But I digress . . .

T. C. SANDERS (*Union of Independent Companies*): I am a small engineering company employer and a member of the Union of Independent Companies. The chairman of one of the committees was invited but unable to come, and his comment on job subsidies was simply that governments rob profitable companies by excessive taxation, thus inhibiting employment and expansion, and then use the money to help create protected jobs, instead of wealth-creating employment. He thinks this typifies bureaucratic absurdity *par excellence*.

In our own company, where we employ only a few people, we have had the opportunity of taking on some of the 'work-experience' candidates. We found that the Department of Employment had to contact the Careers Office or the Department of Education. We had to have a training officer over from the training group of the scheme, who wanted to look at the typewriter! Could the applicant see the accounts? Would she be able to learn the telephone? All this was listed as six months' work for her. And, as a result, we eventually got a candidate—two months later. She was not properly qualified, as she had not been employed for the statutory six months. We took her on. She became reasonably satisfactory. After six months she had a job and the Department was of course highly delighted that this particular 'work experience' had in their view created an additional job. We then found to our utter astonishment that they would pay her £20 a week for the next six months because they reckoned she had been unemployed for the previous six months. So we got even more benefit. This is the way that some of the schemes work at ground level.

I also have another hat to wear as a member of an engineering training group where we trained apprentices—and under the Manpower Services Commission we have special projects for training 16-19 year olds. Vast sums of money are available for this scheme. As a training organisation we thought—and here we agree with Dr Addison—that there was scope for further training of the semi-skilled who have failed to qualify as apprentices. So we went along to the Commission, but they said that the only applicants that were left were the under-achievers, the unemployables, those they really wanted to hand over to the Social Services and Welfare people. They were *really* unemployable, so we were unable to make any contribution there.

My own company is fairly small. We had a very rough time in 1975, but I had a look before I came here at the number of people we employed: in 1976 it was 12 people: we created four more jobs so that it rose to 16 last year, and is now 20. Some of the Union of Independent Companies' proposals state that there are 800,000 small firms and independent companies in Britain, and that if every one of them took on one extra person, it would solve half the unemployment problem at once. We have done our bit—we have gone up from 12 to 20! But we are so small that I think the academics probably overlook us and the politicians have admitted that they do not understand us. If they were to see what it was that motivated us to grow from 12 to 20 people in two years, they would perhaps find out very much more about job creation and the incentive to employ more people.

MR JOHN LEWIS (*Cross Keys College, Gwent*): I would like to take up the point about job creation as a substitute for transfer payments. I think that this approach could be particularly useful where the jobs are highly labour intensive and produce a useful product. The obvious candidate here seems to me to be improvement grants for unfit houses. We could have a programme which might make up for 50 years of rent control and mis-directed subsidies. And I think we would get a useful product. We are told by the trade unions that there are about 300,000 skilled building workers out of work. Those of you who have attempted to get a builder, as I have done, will treat those figures with some scepticism—even more, perhaps, than the strike statistics. But I think we must take it that there *is* at least a pool of trained building workers floating around which could be tapped and put to work on these tasks. The economy would gain a lasting benefit, and we would get the houses improved. There would be a standing deterrent to 'termite' councils to knock them down in the future, because the compensation would be astronomical. And this type of job could be self-liquidating. You are not tying up enormous quantities of capital. You could wind it up fairly quickly if business improved and the construction industry wanted more workers. And you could wind up the improvement grants programme gradually and transfer the workers with little dislocation.

There are probably other labour-intensive job schemes that would be useful.

DR ADDISON: In my view, Mr Sanders's comments and those of an earlier speaker amply demonstrate the problems in designing manpower programmes of this type. I would emphasise that job creation is a complex business the success of which depends crucially on how well the programmes are constructed and funded. And the effect is that these elements have yet to be defined. A detailed answer to the point raised by Mr Lewis is, I think, contained in the first half of my paper. Given this material, my immediate response was to liken his proposal to those employed in an earlier age by Louis Napoleon, who, it will be recalled, cut unemployment at a stroke by getting individuals to dig holes in the Champs de Mars and subsequently to fill them in again. Since the speaker is referring to improvements in the housing stock rather than holes I think I should not pursue the analogy further. And instead simply make a plea for an adequate benefit-cost appraisal.

PROF. D. JOHNSON (*City of London Polytechnic/University of Washington*): My question concerns an argument that the late Harry Johnson used to make and that has been picked up by Herbert Stein in the United States. After you look at the so-called unemployables and some of the imperfections in information you so cogently pointed to, what you really end up with is not involuntary unemployment but totally *voluntary* unemployment, a matter of free choice between work and leisure.

DR ADDISON: The late Professor Harry Johnson also referred, did he not, to the 'mixed-up' economy? This phenomenon has, of course, provided ammunition for those who see in large-scale job subsidies the prospect of achieving a second (or rather n-th) best solution. But, more substantively, I think we should move away from the terms 'voluntary' and 'involuntary', at least as code words respectively denying and supporting the desirability of government intervention in a labour market. Few would argue that all voluntary unemployment is socially beneficial, or that a particular natural rate of unemployment is sancrosanct. Similarly, the involuntarily unemployed may have applied inappropriately for jobs, been searching in the wrong area, or operating with too high a reservation wage. In neither case should we disregard the possibility of efficiency gains. The crucial point to recognise is that if we label unemployment as a problem we must by the same token demonstrate that it implies an inefficiency. This is the real issue.

2 Wage Differentials and Created Employment

MALCOLM R. FISHER

Australian Graduate School of Management,
University of New South Wales

The Author

MALCOLM FISHER: Professor of Economics, Australian Graduate School of Management, University of New South Wales, since 1977. From 1954 to 1977 he was Lecturer in Economics, Director of Studies in Economics and Fellow of Downing College, Cambridge. Member of the Advisory Council of the IEA. Author of *The Economic Analysis of Labour* (1971); *Measurement of Labour Disputes and their Economic Effects* (1974). The IEA has published his *Macro-Economic Models* (Eaton Paper 2, 1964), and two essays: 'Too Little and Too Late?', in *Crisis '75 . . . ?* (Occasional Paper Special (No. 43), 1975); 'Foster Economic Growth', in *Catch '76 . . . ?* (Occasional Paper Special (No. 47), 1976).

I. INTRODUCTION

Must we blame Winston Churchill's enforcement of a return to gold at too high a parity for the intellectual assignment of all our economic ills to the inadequate functioning of the labour market from then on?

Certainly the Government of 1925 imposed upon the British economy too high a wage-cost structure which sustained an already dismal economic performance on to which the Depression of the turn of the 'thirties was grafted. Concern with the performance of the economy in the 'twenties induced Keynes to produce in succession the *Treatise on Money* and his much more influential *General Theory*, works in which the weaknesses of the labour market were assigned central roles. These were depicted in two forms.

In the *Treatise*, whilst demand-led inflation was discussed, attention was also given to what he called incomes inflation (now cost-push), where prices and wages could be simply pushed up by pressure from monopolistic firms or from trade unions provided the monetary authorities were accommodating.[1]

In the *General Theory* the money wage-rate was taken as externally given, with the barest hint that if it moved it would be a consequence of the pressures that are emphasised in the *Treatise*. Now Keynes added to this the empirical observation that it is easier for money wage-rates to be bid up than to go down. No trade union would stand for a cut in its members' money wage-rates, for to accept this within one section of the labour force would be to accept a setback not imposed upon other sections. If wage-rates became too high relative to prices so that full employment was not forthcoming, the only viable policy alternatives would be the raising of the price level, or at least the raising of profit margins through augmented output, each by conscious means, either that of fiscal aid to consumption and investment spending, or by sustained reduction in the interest rate to induce private investment, the power of which stimulus Keynes doubted. Unlike manipulation of wage-rates, this would be equitable in its impact on earners.

---

[1] Malcolm R. Fisher, 'Price and Incomes Policies—Can they Work?', in S. R. Shenoy (ed.), *Wage-Price Control*, Centre for Independent Studies, Turramurra, Australia, 1978.

Keynesian ideas and their grip on economists

These ideas, implanted by Keynes, have had a powerful grip on the economics profession ever since. The American economists took both aspects of the argument over, almost uncritically, it would seem. For there is scant evidence of widespread trade union power on the British scale and certainly what power there has been has diminished. Moreover their output and employment experiences in the 'twenties were substantially different from Britain's and the monetary policies of the Great Depression blatantly so. Yet such was the persuasiveness of Keynes's thought that the differing empirical experiences were thought to be of minor import.

The mechanical models of income determination that were quickly accepted as demonstrating the strength of the Keynesian argument neglected the elements of the product-price/wage-rate structure entirely, but nevertheless Keynes's basic views on the inadequacies of labour markets were built upon and gradually influenced policy. The wage structure itself was claimed to be very rigid, with patterns of differentials exhibiting high stability over time, suggesting the dominance of sociological or traditional elements in their determination. In the spirit of Keynes's emphasis on income flows for correction of unemployment, the roles of individual wage and price adjustment in the re-allocation of economic activity between industries and firms were virtually dismissed. The procrustean nature of the wage structure was taken to mean that wages and prices could be consciously manipulated—through political pressure to change ingrained habits, so as to ensure that full employment policies were not impeded. In this way incomes inflation might be prevented.

Alternatively, where inflation had already occurred, the introduction of a long-term incomes policy would enable the necessary correctives in total spending and employment levels to be carried through without complications. Keynes's chief disciple, Lord Kahn, emphasises such views.[2] On the other hand, James Meade[3] in his Nobel Award lecture, regards fiscal and monetary policies to secure full employment as insufficient when the labour market ceases to

---

[2] Richard Kahn, 'Some Aspects of the Development of Keynes's Thought', *Journal of Economic Litarature*, June 1978.

[3] James Meade, 'The Meaning of "Internal Balance"', *Economic Journal*, September 1978.

perform its allocative functions properly and argues for the spread of arbitral wage-fixing bodies which may be reasonably efficient in bringing about the adjustments that the competitive market is incapable of making for itself.[4]

Manipulation/distortion of the wages structure

The egalitarian arm of the economics profession, building on the presumed social determination of relative wage-rates, has endeavoured to promote schemes for, and encourage policy towards, a re-design of the structure of wage differentials more in line with their own goals, whilst many concerned with the incidence of poverty within the labour force have argued for relatively higher rates of reward for the unskilled as an income corrective measure. The labour market and its reward structure can be manipulated fairly freely, they would claim, to satisfy social goals.

As all of us have so often observed, when inflation escalates governments quite speedily resort time and again to incomes policies, no matter how much doubt is cast upon their success the last time round. Governments cajole union leaders into support, with the latter exerting demands for a range of 'quid pro quos' embracing such features as employment protection, increased compensation for redundancy, various forms of price fixing, commitments to industrial democracy, and so on, so that the wage-rate structure becomes increasingly paralleled by an employment regulatory structure for those lucky enough to serve in firms that remain viable. Not surprisingly to some of us, observed consequences include ever-sharper delineation between workers regularly employed and those frequently unemployed.

It cannot be denied that the labour market has taken a battering.

We single out four main strands of these arguments for critical assessment.

II. FIVE PROPOSITIONS (OR POTENTIAL FALLACIES)

Proposition (Potential Fallacy) 1

The money wage-rate is subject to upwards pressure from trade unions without any effective limit because it is non-economically determined. The determination of money wage-rates is a political

---

[4] If he had seen the Australian Arbitration Commission's performance his enthusiasm for this approach might rapidly diminish.

problem.[5] We take the weaker version where, under fairly fixed exchange rates, money wage-rates rise and with parallel price rises the external trade balance deteriorates—assuming, of course, that money supply moves up proportionately.

That the money wage-rate determination is only a political problem cannot be true for an open economy since, even under flexible exchange rates, there would be a fall in the value of the pound sufficient to compensate for the excess of home over foreign inflation rates at given levels of interest rates. The rising domestic cost of imports has adverse consequences for efficiency and employment and may affect equity also. There is much more than politics involved. The market is not dismissed so easily. But the causation process is far from clear— sustained union militancy may lead to persisting money-wage rises if the monetary authority is accommodating. But such pressures may be applied more subtly. Governments, remembering the inter-war period, have become acutely sensitive to the employment issue and have promoted demand-expansion policies to keep employment rates high. Any excess demand pressure they have introduced through fiscal-money expansion tends to push up money wage-rates and prices.

Created employment and money illusion

This pattern seems to fit much post-war experience and notably the Heath rush to restore employment levels in the early 'seventies. But we then run up against the important Friedman-Phelps proposition[6] that employment expansion is induced only over the range where money wage-rates rise more slowly than prices. As soon as workers become aware that their real wage-rate has been squeezed and press for higher, or at least price-movement-matching, money wage increases, profit margins become eroded and unemployment returns. Such politically-created employment measures rest on money illusion properties that will fairly soon be seen through.

In any event, even in heavily unionised Britain, the origins of trade

---

[5] D. E. Moggridge and S. Howson, 'Keynes on Monetary Policy, 1910-1946', *Oxford Economic Papers*, July 1974, p. 244, note 1, where there is an extract from a letter written by Keynes on this matter.

[6] M. Friedman, 'The Role of Monetary Policy', *American Economic Review*, March 1968; E. S. Phelps (ed.), *Micro-economic Foundations of Employment and Inflation Theory*, Norton Press, New York, 1970.

union pressure on wage-rates are unclear, but in countries with much less unionisation, such as the United States, where similar events have occurred, albeit at a slower pace, governmental concern to keep employment high has probably been an originating factor to which fiscal, and inevitably monetary, expansion have been the crucial accomplices. Since such policies offer only short-term advantages, and inevitable long-term disadvantages, governments should be learning to leave them alone. An election unfortunately arrives in the short term whereas the political legacy is felt in the longer term when a government has acquired a degree of immunity through what statisticians call the high level of 'noise' in the system.

Proposition (Potential Fallacy) 2
The money-wage system containing the set of rewards for a range of occupational and industrial skills sub-divided by sex, age and location is sociologically determined and hence can be altered if sociological reasons for doing so can be advanced. This may have as a corollary that the structure is rather impervious to changing pressures of aggregate demand whether upwards into boom or downwards into slump.

The stability of the wage system has often been attested to but it is less impressive the more closely one examines the material. First, rarely is it made clear whether one is talking about rates, or average earnings per hour, or per week. Relative rigidities within the former are more significant. But even so the 'skill margin' (the ratio between skilled and unskilled wage-rates) has been found to vary significantly between boom when it falls and slump when it rises, though the most recent setback looks as if it could prove an exception.

Stability of differential wage-rates for skills
Supply-demand economists—the despised neo-classicals—have themselves contributed to problems of interpretation of wage structures by suggesting that wage-rates should rise in expanding and decline in contracting industries. Within any skill category that need not be true. If the employment pressures from an expanding industry are exactly counter-balanced by the diminished demands within a contracting industry, wage-rates for the skill will be virtually stable over time, as Joan Robinson has emphasised.[7] Differential movements in rates of

---

[7] Joan Robinson, 'Rising Supply Price', *Economica*, 1941; M. R. Fisher, *Economic Analysis of Labour*, Weidenfeld and Nicolson, 1971, Chapter 8.

pay may emerge as between specialist skills, upward pressures on rates when demand increases for the newer skills, and at best holding conditions on rates when demand recedes for the more obsolete skills. For any one skill we might alternatively argue that both rising and falling demand markets will have to pay the same going wage-rate for the equivalent skill.

On either of these grounds, we should not expect to discover variations in wage structure save across dissimilar skills, the effects of which may be concealed in concocted aggregate skill pay-margin ratios, or in across-industry wage averages where skills are not distinguished.

There are other influences at work to minimise variations in the wage structure over time. Skill pay-margins reflect, *inter alia*, both scarcity of talent and rates of gross return required to compensate for costs of training for higher skill. Substantial variations occurring in the shape of the wage structure would therefore say something quite strong about changes in the rates of return to training on offer. Such unexpected changes would precipitate mobility of existing labour as between skills or encourage new entrants to crowd the higher-rewarded skills after net costs have been taken into account. Further, since for the employer it is efficiency wages, and indeed more generally labour costs, that are important, we cannot insist that the market should primarily move towards effective clearance by altering relative money wage-rates rather than by a system whereby there is effective screening by employers of employees to get better work efficiency for money wage paid when demand for labour falls off and a slackening in such screening when demand improves. It is this last point that I should wish to emphasise in meeting questionable Proposition 3.

If the wage structure can and should be given an economic explanation, as is claimed here—the elements are essential components of an allocation mechanism for the pricing of labour—it bodes ill for the development of an efficient labour force if political measures are taken to compress the structure. At the very least such measures would squeeze the rates of return for the acquisition of skill and this short-fall would have to be met by sufficiently extended employment prospects in the higher skills if investment in skill is to continue at all. Queueing will develop for unskilled jobs, rewards being higher for the successful, but with such labour becoming relatively more costly to employ, and scarcities emerging in the skilled categories. After all, if wage-price rationing is abandoned, quantity rationing is inevitable. Political squeezing of skill margins leads to job queues, a severe embarrassment to politicians. But politicians want to have their cake and eat it. Instead of abandoning their tinkering with wage-rate ratios, they try to bring forward *ad hoc* schemes to disperse job queueing, producing effects just like those from patching a thoroughly worn-out garment.

Proposition (Potential Fallacy) 3
The wage-rate is resistant to downward pressure to a much greater extent than it is resistant to upward pressure, in fact nearly completely so.

The only point, additional to that discussed earlier, I would make here is that when monetary-fiscal expansion policies become the norm it will be rare for wage-rate falls to occur: at the very least they will be strongly outweighed by wage-rate rises. In an open economy where the exchange rate takes the strain, a truer measure of the relevant wage-rate movement over time might be obtained from an index constructed from observations of movements in the money wage-rate corrected in some appropriate way by the exchange rate.

Proposition (Potential Fallacy) 4
Egalitarian and poverty correction schemes can be pursued through the wage structure. A dramatic recent example is the legislative raising of rates of pay for women.

This idea is really an extension of Proposition 2, for it rests on the view that the wage structure can be easily manipulated politically for social ends without unfavourable side-effects. The minimum wage, if set above the market-clearing wage—and if not it does not warrant discussion—can be expected to make the category of labour affected relatively too expensive, so labour shedding will take place. There are arguments that pressures on employers through higher wage costs will induce them to improve their efficiency, but little store can be placed on these. Their effects, if any, will be quickly dissipated. It is far more likely that firms will instal labour-economising techniques, but these, curiously, could involve expansion of labour-absorbing industries. Analysis apart, there is a vast array of evidence to support the view that, when wage-rates are raised in this way, unemployment follows for the categories affected as directly as night follows day.[8]

It seems a very strange social corrective policy for the plight of low earners to offer them higher wage-rates and then deny them the jobs that would give them their incomes! Were it not that politicians and intellectuals (including economists) so often advance these schemes, we would ignore them entirely as obviously nonsensical.

The equal pay scheme for women may strike at discrimination in certain quarters, notably government bodies where the profit motive is dispensed with. In competitive enterprise there seems no reason why the advent of equal pay should induce employers to hire more of an increasingly expensive labour supply. Whether women's earnings in general will suffer so much depends upon the extent of removal of discrimination in the public sector and on the effect of the new composition of market demand on the employment of women in production processes. If demand shifts towards women-employing production industries there will be favourable effects for some women on both pay and employment grounds.

Proposition (Potential Fallacy) 5

Unemployment can be corrected by expansion of fiscal and monetary flows accompanied by expectation of rises in commodity prices that permit higher profit margins, or through volume increases in output which enable overhead costs to be spread and higher profit margins to be realised. In either case the policy measure has to be quite explicit, private enterprise of its own having entered into a situation of under-utilised capacity with which it is claimed to be content.

To this argument, the nub of Keynes's *General Theory*, we devote the balance of this paper. The emphasis now turns to employment but the role of the wage structure in promoting employment and output is, as a rule, dismissed. The discussion brings us hard up against the issue of market *versus* government employment, or productive *versus* created employment (the new and the originally proposed titles of this Seminar). These references are broader than Proposition 5 itself, but it is worth spending a short time examining the more general issues they raise.

---

[8] J. Mincer, 'Unemployment Effects of Minimum Wages', *Journal of Political Economy*, August 1976; F. Welch, 'Minimum Wage Legislation in the United States', *Economic Enquiry*, September 1974.

III. JOB CREATION AND RATIONAL CHOICE

Created employment suggests activity is being generated that no-one in his wildest dreams would pursue for rational reasons. This shifts the ground to a discussion of rational choice. Employment can take place only in the presence of, and through the action of, employers—whether private firms or governmental undertakings. Whether single entrepreneur, partnership, private or public company, all firms have one common characteristic—they must have made, be making, or be expected to make, net profits with a strong enough place in the market to be able to ride an uncomfortable fall in demand for their product; or, if they are new firms, they must know that their survival will before long be assessed in the same terms. Whether they maximise profits or not is immaterial: they must, on average, over a period reduce costs and make a surplus, or cease to exist. Quite a number in practice fail to pass this test and their guiding entrepreneurs suffer periods of low output and bankruptcy.

Such adjustments may be difficult to observe but are nevertheless real. Behind the facade of a well-known firm a new venture may be born—there may be no easy way of recognising the death of the old and the birth of the new. To the extent that entrepreneurs cannot easily be identified independently of their enterprises, tracking of their lifetime career paths may not be easy to discern. Yet new entrepreneurs face such information costs in assessing potential. Like existing entrepreneurs they have to weigh the market in forming a judgement on whether it can offer them the profit necessary for survival. Their ability to 'get it right' increases their confidence and also that of their financiers if they are dependent upon outside funds. These judgements on market potential for product, both by type and scale, directly affect their demand for inputs including labour. Moreover, the same process is repeated again and again. Hence suppliers of labour on a regular basis must judge their own prospects of survival within a frame of reference that recognises rather similar criteria.

Government's role in 'public goods'

Government differs from private enterprise through its ability to exercise powers of coercion in directions that it can represent as furthering the 'public good'. Its coercive powers extend from the right to tax, police or regulate to its powers to control the scale and working of the monetary system and the degree of participation in international trade. Government has the power to curtail activity in

49

the decentralised sector with its non-loss-making rationale to the point where it may decide to perform activities such as the private sector would no longer perform in its own right or in which the market system is believed to be ill-suited to work efficiently.

From Adam Smith to the present day, it seems to be generally accepted that there are goods and services that decentralised decision-taking would under-provide, though conjointly people would be eager to provide, for example those of national or civil defence. With such 'public goods' coercion would seem essential for efficient scale of provision, but such coercion has a price which the community might not wish to pay since it involves curtailment of what would normally be provided through the decentralised sector. There are certain necessaries that people will not be willing to forego, even in the interests of national defence. There is no point in being protected if you cannot survive in a tolerable way—and the essentials for survival can be satisfied through private initiative and decentralised markets. Beyond such limited cases as defence the argument for searching scrutiny is reinforced, especially as some of the proposed activities inevitably involve operating at a loss.

Is government an efficient entrepreneur?
Any comparison of institutions should include a discussion of efficiency in which the question of monitoring activities should be squarely faced. In private enterprise the single entrepreneur or the shareholders in public companies fill the role and bear the consequences of inefficiency, but with government undertakings the incentive structure is lax and ineffective. The risks of failure of enterprise have a bearing on performance of employees.

If government is going to create employment it must know that, on average and over time, it will not make a loss, otherwise that activity will not long survive; or it must recognise that it can finance any sustained losses only by squeezing the activities of individuals, or firms which have in the main enjoyed good prospects of breaking even. It may of course believe that it can goad the decentralised sector into activities that it would not otherwise have undertaken, acting as a kind of 'booster' of confidence, a sort of 'psychological public good'. Or it may merely believe that it can make gestures of this type which accord it temporary support from which it can conveniently withdraw when the expected benefits are no longer thought to matter. If these powers exist, we may wonder why they have not already been used to more effect, instead of letting decentralised activity ebb to a level where it gives politicians cause for concern. And indeed, why has not a sufficient degree of counter-pessimism been dispensed when the economy has become over-exuberant? May it be that these confidence-generating powers are unlikely to deceive people for long, so that the depressive effects set in almost immediately whether or not they are self-cancelling? If confidence-creating powers are available, why should we have to experience periodic short-falls in activity at all?

The length of time over which such boosting of confidence may be expected to persist is relevant to judgement on 'temporary support'. But we must then ask where such transitory activity fits within the long-term strategy of government. Do awkward 'hollows' in government planning, and action, require such filling operations; or does the need for such action throw into sharp relief some deep-seated fault in the design and execution of government programmes? Unless these questions can be answered positively it seems unlikely that the community will favour financing such operations at the expense of decentralised activity subject to market test.

IV. FINANCING EFFECT ON PRIVATE SECTOR INVESTMENT

Created employment in the private sector requires explicit subsidy to individuals or firms. Whether the creation is within the private or government sector, it must be financed by taxes, by issue of debt absorbed by central banks through monetary expansion, or by bonds sold to individuals and firms at higher interest rates that impinge upon the financing costs for alternative borrowing, and inventory financing, by firms. Such created activity may also serve to displace activity in the private sector directly, but any of these methods of financing make it more difficult for output to be sustained in the decentralised sector and serve to eliminate new projects.

Created employment that is the response to elimination of jobs caused, say, through mistakenly depressive monetary policies may not have this drawback, but here it is clear that the right medicine is simply the reversal of the erroneous policy.

Created employment has implications for factor markets. Through higher financing costs labour employed on other projects may be discharged. The net gain in labour employed will be less than the explicit employment-creation project would indicate. But these projects involve team effort; hence other skills already in demand will be raided for these schemes with rising wage-rates confronting all employers of the skills affected. Such schemes are, of course, designed to reduce the pools of unemployed and therefore should draw labour primarily from those sources. But if they are designed with that specifically in mind they are likely to enjoy merely transitory government support. As soon as the numbers unemployed in these critical groupings of skills are substantially reduced, the projects will tend to be phased out. But is this the sort of treatment that should be meted out to these workers? There is at that stage no guarantee that workers on such projects will be readily absorbed elsewhere. Those employed on created projects have probably not had their work well monitored—short-term schemes of job creation seem to be speedily assembled without adequate supervision and poor incentive structures. The recent Fifth Report of the Committee of Public Accounts bears strong testimony to this.[9] The point is reinforced when we note that many of the unemployed for whom the jobs were created are in that predicament partly as a result of tighter monitoring arrangements introduced by private firms as recession deepens. Again, where training has been given on temporary projects it is vital for improved chances of re-employment that workers acquire skills that are versatile in developing industries. The risk of such people being induced to persist with outdated skills is a real one.

Inflationary effects of created employment
Created employment schemes of any type, including the stimulus given directly to enterprise through more relaxed money-fiscal policies, will create employment in the short run but as bottlenecks emerge will add to inflation. Money illusion will wear off, and the Friedman-Phelps point that unemployment will re-emerge, but *at a higher rate of inflation*, holds true. Insofar as the created expansion draws heavily on already scarce factors, the inflation barrier will be hit sooner. Such created employment policies, then, have at best a place in periods of real depression and under conditions where

---

[9] Committee of Public Accounts, *5th Report: Session 1977-78*, HC 573, HMSO, 1978.

inflation psychology has not become really deep-seated. Even Keynes was more sensitive about their use than many contemporary economists who invoke his support.[10]

Government intervention and economic oscillations
We would not dispute that a world experiencing structural change will exhibit oscillations in output and employment. But we believe that many of the oscillations experienced are attributable to excessive government intervention in the economy. If the extent of intervention were to be eased, some of the observed oscillations would also vanish. Such excessive government intervention can impose strain on the efficiency of labour markets, and increase unemployment rather than reduce it. Sir John Hicks tells us in his *The Crisis in Keynesian Economics*, that from 1914 he is impressed by the rigidity of the wages structure, with 1920-23, years of sharp rises in prices and wage-rates followed immediately by a dramatic fall, standing out as exceptions.[11] Are we misled by words? Could one not as easily say that the years 1920-23 were years of exceptional flexibility in wage-rates? Furthermore, no-one has addressed the question of how to determine whether the wage system is sufficiently flexible for effective functioning. In this paper we have tried to show some of the strengths of its economic rationale whilst pointing out the limits in internal flexibility that would be consistent in any event with a competitive market. The so-called inadequacies of the labour market may to no small extent be due to a combination of a biased reading of evidence coupled with an over-active government corrective policy.

If alternatively this view is dismissed as too conservative, we are at least entitled to ask whether the remedies proposed will help the disadvantaged. We have advanced strong reasons why this may not be so. Moreover, the effects of a sequence of incomes policies has been to add rigidity to the employment structure both directly and indirectly *via* the deals done to ensure acquiescence of the trade

---

[10]Contrast J. M. Keynes's article in the *Melbourne Herald*, 25 May 1932 (reproduced in E. O. G. Shann and D. B. Copland, *The Australian Price Structure, 1932*, Angus and Robertson, Sydney, 1933), with the policy recommendations in T. Balogh *et al.*, *Economics of Full Employment*, Basil Blackwell, Oxford, 1944, and with almost all widely-used macro-economic texts even up to the present.

[11]John Hicks, *The Crisis in Keynesian Economics*, Section III, Oxford, 1974.

unions. In times of adversity we know all firms expect to prune their labour forces, but they do cling to those employees who have been specifically trained at employer's cost, to those used in close association with retained capital, and to those whom, if let go now, it would be difficult to replace later.[12] Firms are also saddled with other workers whom unions want retained on some seniority criterion of their own, and also by legislation they are forced to square up to the extra costs imposed if they dismiss anybody. Such an assemblage serves to increase the rigidity of the wage-employment structure in the short run whilst ensuring that if slump deepens the oscillations in the wage-employment nexus will become more dramatic later. To mitigate the concentrated unemployment that results amongst the unskilled and the young, employment-creating rather than surplus-generating schemes are adopted. But wherever chosen the beneficial effects will be short run.

V. CONCLUSION

The forms of correction resorted to seem to be leading us into a *cul-de-sac*. There is a strong case for the opposite strategy. This would require that government should place its emphasis on improving the background rules and pre-conditions for the functioning of markets and the working of the monetary system. In this way the existing degree of flexibility in labour and product markets will be deployed to promote the growth of output, the best insurance of good employment prospects.

Questions and Discussion

DR RICHARD LAYARD (*London School of Economics*): I agree with a good bit of what Malcolm Fisher has said about the long-run operation of the economy. But I would like to make one point about a cyclical problem. It seems to me that there are essentially three ways in which an economy could deal with a slump. One, it could spontaneously emerge from it. Secondly, the government could create some jobs of its own

---

[12]M. R. Fisher, F. M. Gruen, P. Sheehan, D. Stammer, *Real Wages and Unemployment*, Centre for Applied Economic Research, University of New South Wales, No. 4, March 1978.

temporarily, which Professor Fisher has focussed on; or thirdly, it could subsidise employment in the private sector.

I think there is a role for government intervention. But it has not been emphasised sufficiently that where the government should intervene is in the parts of the economy which have suffered the downturn. So I would accept Professor Fisher's argument that there is something to be said against creating temporary jobs in the public sector which are going to be abandoned when the recovery comes. If the main downturn in activity has occurred in the private sector, that seems to me to constitute the main argument for trying to stimulate activity in the private sector, and is the main argument for using job subsidies rather than public sector jobs as the counter-slump weapons. The difficulty is in identifying those parts of the downturn which are permanent because they are connected with the decline of industries, and those which are temporary. But I think that it is essentially the case, which I do not feel that he sufficiently dealt with, that if stimulating activity is directed to the sectors which have suffered downward shock, it is not obvious that it has the inflationary consequences I think he was trying to make us worry about.

I would like to make one other point about his proposition—Fallacy Four—where he was talking about money wage rigidity. The real issue is whether it is true that in slumps the real wage goes up. That is essentially what he wants us to believe—that a slump arises because the real wage has gone too high. But we all know that if you measure the real wage in the normal way it goes *down* in a slump. And this is the fundamental argument against his way of looking at the source of cyclical movements in employment.

Then he wants us to say: 'Oh, but that's an illusion. It does not really go down. What happens is that the quality of labour has gone up and if you had really held the quality of labour constant you would have found that the real wage goes up.' I have just been doing some sums which I will not bore you with, but it seems to me inconceivable that, given the amount by which we know real wages do go down in slumps relative to trend, you could show that in practice the real wage per constant unit of labour had gone up. I do not think that is a viable model of the labour market.

DR BARRY BRACEWELL-MILNES (*Erasmus University, Rotterdam*): I would like to make a comment on both the first two speakers. A lot of this morning's discussion has concerned the question of the 'second best', to use what is both the technical term and the popular term for what you do in an unsatisfactory situation. And the argument for 'job creation' has usually been presented in a second-best sense; for example, perhaps the public sector borrowing requirement will fall rather than rise, although we have had two different opinions even on that. What we have not had so far is the comment that this second-best argument has itself a hidden cost which ought to be brought out into the open, which is something we try to do with other hidden costs.

One of the advantages of the sad economic performance of this country over the last five years or more has been the discrediting of the orthodoxies of the 'forties, 'fifties and 'sixties. We should not have reached the stage where people are so sceptical, had not the degree of mismanagement been such that the truth was beginning to be unavoidable even to those who did not wish to look at it. Yet if the second-best approach had been more successful during the last five or 10 years, the public (and perhaps some of us) might have gone on deluding themselves for longer about the existence of fairy gold, thereby concealing the degree of economic mismanagement.

The same kind of criticism can be applied not only to the management of the economy but also to smaller-scale operations. One speaker, for example, made a special case for a form of job creation directed towards the improvement of the housing stock. If we had this form of job creation it might distract our attention and that of the public from the fact that the present shortage of housing is due to government mismanagement, since rent controls were introduced in 1916. And it is a cost that second-best arguments distract both the public and professionals from the main lines of the argument. When you add that to what we have already heard this morning, that the second-best arguments are often debatable and that the balance of advantage is ambiguous in direction, it seems to me to amount to a very strong case against second-best arguments in a number of spheres which are relevant to our discussion today.

RALPH HARRIS (*Chairman*): I hope the last speaker's doubts were reinforced by our first platform speaker saying, if I heard correctly, that some intervention would be justified by anticipated export gains that were measured by 0.2 to 0.3 per cent of the GNP. I do not know whether to admire most his mathematics or his faith in that kind of calculation, which seems to me invisible to the naked eye.

PROF. D. JOHNSON: I would like to ask Professor Fisher if he believes, like Professor Friedman, that the inflation problem is in principle very easy to solve technically, but difficult to solve as a political problem, since government officials for all kinds of reasons look at the short-run transitional costs that seem to them very high. Would he consider as a proposal of second best one of Friedman's proposals, namely a move towards indexation of wages and prices so as to mitigate the transitional movement to a lower rate of inflation?

PROF. FISHER: I will take the questions in reverse order. It is fascinating, after being so heavily involved in British economic discussion for a quarter of a century, suddenly to be so recently translated to Australia and all its problems—the last speaker triggered something off in the Australian context. I have never, in print or in any other way, advocated indexation. I have never been keen on that Friedman line at all, and to the extent that I ever toyed with it, I would toy with it less now. In Australia in 1973, the government of the day, for various reasons which may conceivably have a longer-run economic justification than they are given credit for, sub-stantially increased the role of the public sector and in particular raised public-sector wages enormously. That might indeed be a reason I now live in Australia, because academics benefited enormously. But the mood was developing that, with inflation accelerating, indexation should be introduced—and I think it was the present Prime Minister who introduced it quite sensibly into tax structures. Then it was extended rather speedily to the wage structure after the wage level had been shifted up to such an unduly high level, through public sector stimulation!

So the Australian economy was saddled with this wretched indexation when the wage-price ratio had been raised seriously out of line, and it now gets 'locked in' to contemporary discussion in Australia, in what is called the 'real wage overhang', unattractive as that terminology may be.

Now either Friedman was not explicit on this aspect or his views were misinterpreted. I have not studied his argument sufficiently. Certainly if you were at the appropriate time to introduce indexation in *all* things, this would clearly reveal to governments the futility of inflation. But the argument has been pulled out of context and used to imply that if at any moment you introduce indexation, something desirable will happen. I have just described sufficiently dramatically the 'something desirable' that did not happen.

Second-best solutions

I am not sure that I can answer Dr Bracewell-Milnes specifically. I did not think I had made anywhere in my paper an argument for second-best solutions. I think I dismissed them *holus bolus*. But I think we must be very careful about dismissing any apparent departures. If you have, say, in Britain a substantial squeeze on the money supply, because inflation has been high—the government taking counter-action, as Mr Healey did in 1974—and some of the marginal banks are getting into liquidity crises, that is simply a crazy policy—you will have liquidation effects which are really severe, and government-imposed. In that situation the correct counter-policy is to expand the money supply somewhat. In other words, if you overdo it, then the corrective is to underdo it. If I moved into the Bank of England tomorrow and applied an unduly tight squeeze on the economy, I should rapidly be dismissed and somebody else would counter the policy immediately.

No economist is arguing that you can be cavalier about these things. Some very untoward effects can be produced by unduly harsh movements in money and fiscal policy. So in that sense you might get very close to a second-best situation, but you are really counteracting an imposed second best in its own terms, and I think economists have got to entertain such possibilities. The point I want to make—and I think it really does need underlining, because our views are heavily misinterpreted from time to time—is that if you trigger off an undue depression, you must take the necessary measures to counter that excessive depression. There is an appropriate policy, and at government level the cumulative depressive effect can easily be overdone.

The ideas that I and others are presenting are continually being dismissed or pooh-poohed on grounds that are quite inappropriate—and we may have laid ourselves open to attack. You have given me the opportunity this morning to show that the point has been well taken.

Private sector job subsidies
Dr Layard raised the question about subsidisation of employment in the private sector. Of course we are all concerned about prolonged unemployment. There is no lack of compassion around regardless of philosophic viewpoint. But compassion without resource is not much good, and one of my general theses was to say that excessive government intervention may produce the untidy and uncomfortable effects which have been described. And I agree that the problem for the disadvantaged in the private sector, as Dr Layard described it, may be the most severe. Of course they may be the unfortunate victims of interactive effects running across industry, rather than from those imposed directly on their own industry. But how do we help them?

Now Sir John Hicks, in his book *The Crisis in Keynesian Economics*, investigated this subject and suggested that corrective schemes of the fiscal type should be directed to where the multiplier effects are greatest, that is, to those where labour is heavily unemployed and there is no strong dependence on supporting inputs, so that inflation does not build up in the prices of co-operant factors. My own view is that it is very difficult to single out such areas, and since fine-tuning is already in the dock, under such policies it will be in the dock even more often. But even if you have expansion that starts there, where do you contain it? Because, since capacity is utilised there, unless the tap is very carefully turned off, activity will spread very quickly elsewhere. So the people you are trying to help may benefit in the short run and be damaged in the long run. If people in the private sector are damaged and the initially cyclical effect is supported by a permanent decline, then what is required above all is awareness of the need for flexibility and the facility to provide labour with alternative training opportunities. And the shock effect now imposed should be a means of encouragement to them both directly and indirectly to secure adjustment to more rewarding markets.

I do not know whether I have answered Dr Layard directly, but I am very doubtful about corrective effects employed in such private sector schemes. They seem to me essentially limited in range. The multiplier effects, if they occur, spill over and the inflationary psychology is generated that soon spreads to other associated industries. A lot of the unemployed would be more directly relieved by less participative government activity overall, and to the extent that they have particular problems, it is critically one of flexibility. The arguments that I have applied in connection with job-creation schemes for the unemployed would apply just as strongly to them.

I come to Dr Layard's second question where he asks whether it is true that real wages go up in slumps. I believe that this question may be pushing me into arguments that I did not intend to make, but let me discuss it in context. A slump may be brought on by a decrease in foreign demand; but if it is purely internally generated it must be associated with a sizeable squeeze on profits and generally on profit margins. As demand diminishes (as I argued in my paper), commodity and product prices are likely to fall much more rapidly than wage-rates, which may continue to rise in money terms under the influence of the preceding boom. Real wage-rates for those still employed may therefore continue to rise in the early part of a slump, and, in index number terms, this rise may conceal some fall in labour costs as firms take the opportunity to regroup up their labour force to obtain more productivity (that is, quality) from monies expended. Earnings will, of course, fall off as overtime is cut and bonus elements are curtailed. For the unskilled the loss in employment far exceeds the rate of fall in money wage-rates if these fall absolutely at all.

These points would also be relevant to the Keynes-Dunlop-Tarshis debate about the inter-dependence of real wage movements and employment, an issue that, to my knowledge, is still far from resolution.

RALPH HARRIS: It is a shame to draw this session to an end when the Professor is in such a good flow. Could we thank Professor Fisher for coming back from Australia for this occasion and for his fine exposition? (*Applause.*)

3 Trade Unions and Productivity: Job Preservation by American Unions

ALBERT REES
*Princeton University and National
Bureau of Economic Research*

The Author

ALBERT REES: Professor of Economics and Public Affairs, Princeton University, since 1966. Formerly taught at the University of Chicago, 1948-66, where he became Professor of Economics in 1961. He is author of *Real Wages in Manufacturing, 1890-1914* (1960); *The Economics of Trade Unions* (1961).

Since this paper was presented, he has become President of the Alfred P. Sloan Foundation.

I. INTRODUCTION

The creation of new jobs to expand employment and the preservation of old jobs to prevent a decline in employment are in some sense opposite sides of the same coin. In the United States, the Federal government has been the sponsor of 'job creation programmes', while trade unions have been responsible for 'job preservation' practices.

The practices discussed in this paper are called 'working rules' by the unions and frequently 'restrictive work practices' or 'feather-bedding' by employers and the general public. These rules are of three principal types:

(i) crew size rules, which specify the minimum number of workers that can be used to do a particular task or to staff a particular piece of equipment;

(ii) rules requiring unnecessary work to be done; and

(iii) jurisdictional or demarcation rules, which specify that certain work can be done only by designated workers.

II. TRADE UNION 'WORKING RULES'

Overstaffing and restriction of output do not occur solely in jobs covered by trade unions and collective bargaining. There is a widespread tendency for workers who do repetitive and uninteresting work to value their jobs only for the pay and for the companionship of fellow-workers and not for any interest in the work itself. This leads to a general inclination of such workers to restrict output and to take as much leisure on the job as possible.[1] In the absence of trade unions, such informal restrictive practices can usually be kept within tolerable bounds by management, which would certainly not retain workers who did no work at all. Union work-rules, however, can require that workers be paid for doing nothing.

The painter and the engineer who fished: an illustration

When I served on the Construction Industry Stabilisation Committee, I encountered a situation in which a contractor hired union painters

---

[1] This tendency has been recognised for many years: Stanley B. Mathewson, *Restriction of Output among Unorganised Workers*, Viking Press, New York, 1931.

to paint a highway bridge across a river. The union agreement required that a small boat should patrol the river underneath the bridge to rescue any painter who might fall off, although the usual method of dealing with this hazard would be to rig a net beneath the bridge. Needless to say, the boat was manned by a union painter. However, the boat had an outboard motor, and the jurisdictional rules of the building trades do not permit a painter to operate an engine. A second member of the boat crew was added for this purpose: a union 'operating engineer'. The employer paid skilled craft wage-rates to both workers, and complained that he was never even given any of the fish they caught!

The problem of restrictive work-rules is not uniformly distributed across American industry. On the contrary, it is largely confined to a few industries in which unions are organised along craft rather than industrial lines. Industrial unions often set minimum staffing requirements for certain equipment, but they tend to be set at the plant rather than as national or area standards, and they are much more subject to modification through local negotiation.

The industries where restrictive work practices have a substantial impact include rail and water transport, entertainment, and printing. Restrictive practices have a less severe impact in some aspects of construction and air transport. For reasons to be discussed later, the severity of the problem seems to be decreasing in some of these industries. We shall begin our discussion with railroads.

Attrition (non-replacement) of locomotive firemen
One of the principal collective bargaining issues in railroads has been the staffing or 'crew consist' of trains. From 1935 to 1972 there was a long and acrimonious dispute between the railroads and the Brotherhood of Locomotive Firemen and Enginemen (now part of the United Transportation Union) over whether a fireman (helper) was needed on diesel locomotives in freight service. This dispute was finally settled, after repeated government intervention, by an agreement to eliminate such diesel firemen through attrition by not replacing workers who retire. Disputes are still in progress on the appropriate size of train crews other than engine crews (brakemen and conductors). There are also some staffing issues in the employment of non-operating employees, including railway clerks. A dispute over the demarcation of work between clerks and supervisors caused a long strike on the Norfolk and Western Railroad last summer. This

strike has been suspended during an inquiry by a board appointed by the Federal government.

Crew size was once widely governed by state laws, known as 'full-crew-laws', which required train crews of specified numbers of workers. By 1973, only two states had such statutes.[2]

Another major form of job protection in the railroad unions is the assignment of types of work to particular groups of workers, even within the same craft. For example, a railroad crew that did any switching or setting out or picking up of cars because railyard crews or engines were not available used to receive an additional day's pay for each day such work was done. To avoid such payments, railroads often maintained yard crews even where they could not be kept fully employed. These rules were modified in the early 1970s to permit road crews to do some switching and to merge road and yard seniority lists.[3]

'Property rights' in jobs

The concept that work 'belongs' to particular workers even where other workers are equally qualified to do it established a kind of 'property right' in jobs. It arises historically from two kinds of experience—depressions in which work is generally scarce, and technological change, which sometimes makes craft skills obsolete. The union whose members' skills are threatened may try to delay technological change by making it expensive, or it may insist that its members be given the (exclusive) chance to learn the skills required by the new technology.[4]

Another important aspect of railroad work-rules is that the distance between seniority divisions is generally 100 miles, the length of a day's run many years ago. Although the railroads have won the right to make some inter-divisional runs, the rules still require ex-

---

[2] Robert C. Lieb, *Labor in the Transportation Industries*, Praeger Publishers, New York, 1974, p. 4.

[3] Robert W. Koditek, 'Railroad Companies and the Operating Crafts: The Work Rule Controversy Since 1945', unpublished MBA thesis, New York University, 1978, pp. 7-10.

[4] A conspicuous recent example of the second strategy has been the policy of the International Typographical Union concerning the change from linotype machines to computerised typesetting.

cessive changes of crews and the maintenance of unnecessary stations.[5]

A rough measure of the effect of union work-rules on labour costs in railroads can be obtained by examining the performance of a small railroad, the Florida East Coast, that uses non-union labour. In 1975, its revenue-ton-miles per employee were about 12 per cent higher than those of all Class I railroads.[6] Part of this difference may be due to differences in the composition of traffic and the length of hauls, and to the fact that the Florida East Coast has no passenger service, rather than being due to work-rules. It is likely, however, that economies of scale would cause a small railroad to have *lower* productivity than the average.

Further evidence of the effect of union work-rules is provided by the experience of the Norfolk and Western during the 1978 strike. The railroad was able to maintain most of its service by using supervisory workers only, achieving substantially higher than normal levels of output per hour worked.

Employer avoidance of trade union restrictions

Union work-rules have not prevented employment in rail transport from declining. Total employment in the railroad industry fell from 1,200,000 in 1952 to about 540,000 at the end of 1977. All of this decline in employment resulted from an increase in productivity, since output has risen slightly over the period despite intensive competition from other forms of transport. This growth in productivity resulted partly from new technology, and partly from the substitution of capital for labour, which may be induced by union work-rules. Thus a rule specifying a larger train crew than is required encourages railroad management to run longer trains. If the rule relates the size of the crew to the number of cars in the train, management is encouraged to raise tons per car by investing in larger cars and more powerful locomotives.

Disputes over work-rules are less pervasive in air transport than in railroads. The most important recent disputes have concerned the minimum number of pilots. The Airline Pilots Association requires United Air Lines to use three pilots on the Boeing 737, a two-engine

---

[5] Koditek, *op. cit.*, pp. 14-16.
[6] Computed from data in the annual report of the Florida East Coast Railroad and Moody's transportation manual.

jet aircraft seating 90 to 100 passengers. Similar planes such as the Douglas DC-9 and the BAC 1-11 have only two pilots, and the Federal Aviation Administration has certified the B-737 for operation with two pilots. Crew cost per mile for United's B-737s is substantially higher than competitors' costs for DC-9s. This union practice has sharply limited the use of the B-737 in the United States.[7]

There have also been important work-rule issues in marine transport. The International Longshoremen's Association on the East Coast has regulated the size of longshore crews and the maximum weight of loads on slings. Seafaring unions have requirements for the minimum size of ships' crews, which not only add to wage costs but require additional space on the ship for crew accommodation. American flag shipping is reimbursed for such costs in most cases by government subsidies on some international routes and by the legal prohibition of foreign competition on domestic routes. These include traffic between Hawaii, Alaska and Puerto Rico and the 48 contiguous mainland states. The costs are nevertheless paid by American taxpayers and consumers.

'Dead horse': make-work practices in newspaper printing
Another industry where union working rules often require overstaffing is newspaper publishing. The most famous 'make-work' practice of the printing trades was that of the typographers' union requiring the reproduction of local advertisements received as matrices prepared in other printing establishments, which could be used for printing without setting type. Many 'locals' (printing house branches) of the International Typographical Union long required such work to be reset after it had already appeared in the paper, a practice known as 'bogus' or 'dead horse'. By 1959, only 110 of 558 local typographical unions said they still followed this practice.[8]

A more pressing current issue in newspaper collective bargaining

---

[7] The early history of this dispute is documented in D. Daryl Wyckoff and David H. Maister, *The Domestic Airline Industry*, D. C. Heath, Lexington, Mass., 1977, Chapter 8. Jet operating statistics are from *Air Transport World*, July 1978.

[8] Robert D. Leiter, *Featherbedding and Job Security*, Twayne Publishers, New York, 1964, p. 156. No more recent information is available.

concerns the size of press crews on automated high-speed newspaper presses. A dispute over the staffing of such equipment resulted in a strike that closed the major daily newspapers in New York City from early August to early November of 1978. In settling the strike, the newspapers agreed to guarantee jobs for six years to all 1,500 pressmen. In return, they won the right to reduce the number of pressmen by attrition, through not replacing workers who retire. It is estimated that the number of pressmen will be reduced 30 per cent by 1984.[9]

Restrictions in entertainment: 'standby musicians'

Working rules also have a major impact in entertainment. 'Locals' of the American Federation of Musicians have long set minimum sizes of bands or orchestras; these limits are unrelated to artistic criteria. They also have required 'standby musicians' to be engaged at performances by amateur musicians or by travelling musicians from other areas. The standby musicians are paid whether or not they perform.

On three occasions in the 1930s and 1940s Congress enacted legislation designed to prevent unions from requiring the employment of workers who do no work. Some of this legislation was specifically directed against the musicians' union. The courts effectively nullified the legislation by ruling that, if the workers are willing to work, the law has not been violated. Standby musicians may thus offer to play during intermissions, an offer that might be accepted at a dance, but seldom at a concert.

Craft demarcation in the construction industry

Staffing requirements have not been a major issue in construction. They are most frequently specified for operating engineers, where collective bargaining agreements often state the number of pieces of small equipment, such as compressors, that can be tended by one worker. Jurisdiction or craft demarcation is a much more important issue. For example, an electrician instals a wire box, but a carpenter must make an opening in the wall to permit a wire box to be installed.

'When the work of one trade is incidental, as, for example, when a carpenter must be assigned to only a few minutes work so that the

---

[9] *New York Times*, 7 November, 1978, p. 50.

electrician may proceed (or *vice versa*), the employer may incur great expense.'[10]

Non-union construction contractors have been gaining ground recently. Part of their advantage lies in lower wages, except for the most skilled craftsmen. An important part, however, consists of the ability to assign workers to any work available if they are not required in their specialty. This lowers labour costs even when wages are not below the union rates.

There are also instances in which construction unions insist on performing on site work that could be done more economically in a factory. It is difficult to get current measures of the importance of such practices; my impression is that it is diminishing.

New employer militancy

I have mentioned earlier two major strikes of 1978 that arose out of union work-rules—the New York newspaper strike and the Norfolk and Western Railroad strike. Such strikes are unusual in recent American experience. Employers have not generally considered work-rules as strike issues. They have often tried to eliminate such rules during the renegotiation of contracts by 'buying them out'—that is, by offering higher wages in return for less costly work-rules. Where such efforts have not succeeded, however, employers have usually continued to live with over-staffing and demarcation. What explains this new employer militancy?

I suggest two answers. One is that union strength in the private sector of the American economy is declining. Union membership as a proportion of non-agricultural employment has been falling gradually for many years, and it would have fallen much faster were it not for the rapid growth of unions in the public sector. In manufacturing, mining, construction, and retailing the decline of union strength has been substantial. In manufacturing, for example, reported union membership declined from 8.8 million in 1956 to 8.5 million in 1976. This is a decline from 51 to 45 per cent of total employment in manufacturing, and from 66 to 62 per cent of production worker employment.[11] Along with this decline in strength has gone a less favourable public opinion towards unions, and the defeat

---

[10]Daniel Quinn Mills, *Labor-Management Relations*, McGraw-Hill, New York, 1978, p. 276.
[11]Computed from data of the US Bureau of Labor Statistics.

of national labour legislation that unions have strongly supported. This atmosphere of eroding union strength makes employers bolder.

The second force supporting the elimination of restrictive work-rules is that non-union competition often makes it imperative for union employers to hold down labour costs in order to keep the markets for their products. Such competition may come from within the United States or from imports. Domestic competition from non-union coal-mines and contractors has been important in coal-mining and in construction; import competition has been important in manufacturing. The decline of restrictive work practices in union construction is in my opinion directly related to the growth of non-union contractors in parts of the industry where they were not previously present.

III. GOVERNMENT POLICY ON JOB CREATION

Recent public policy in the United States has fostered job creation for the unemployed through Federal programmes. Advocates of such job-creation programmes might also be expected to favour job preservation through union work-rules. A moment's reflection suggests that the two kinds of employment are not really alike. Federal government programmes have supported the provision of services to the public in the local government and non-profit sectors. Some of these are services that would not otherwise have been provided. These schemes have been part of a macro-economic stimulus package designed to reduce total unemployment; as such they have been paid for from deficit financing by the Federal government.

There may be disagreement over whether this is a better way to increase total employment during recessions than tax reductions that would expand private employment, but there is little question that the programmes do produce an increase in total employment, at least in the short run.

IV. ECONOMIC EFFECTS: JOB CREATION OR REDISTRIBUTION

Jobs preserved by union work-rules may permit the continued employment of particular groups of workers, but there is no assurance whatever that this maintains total employment. The costs of these rules must be passed on by employers in the cost of the goods and services they sell, or absorbed in lower returns on invested capital.

Higher prices or lower dividends leave customers and stockholders with less money to spend on other goods and services. The effect on total employment is therefore much smaller than the number of jobs preserved. Whether it is a positive or negative effect depends on the labour intensity of production in the affected sectors. If consumers must pay more for the services of a capital-intensive, high-wage industry like railroad transport, and have less to spend on all other goods and services, the effect is more likely to be a reduction in total employment than an increase.

Job preservation policies may preserve jobs for present incumbents, although even this effect is not inevitable. *For workers as a whole, they merely redistribute jobs in a way that reduces total output.* Whatever their historical causes, the effect of restrictive work-rules on the welfare of the whole society seems to be unambiguously detrimental.

REFERENCES

Horowitz, Morris A., *Manpower Utilization in the Railroad Industry* (Boston: Northwestern University), 1960.

Kaufman, Jacob J., *Collective Bargaining in the Railroad Industry* (New York: King's Crown Press), 1954.

Leiter, Robert D., *Featherbedding and Job Security* (New York: Twayne Publishers), 1964.

Slichter, Sumner H., James J. Healy and E. Robert Livernash, *The Impact of Collective Bargaining on Management* (Washington: The Brookings Institution), 1960, Chapter 11.

Weinstein, Paul A., *Featherbedding and Technological Change* (Boston: D. C. Heath), 1965.

Questions and Discussion

RALPH HARRIS (*Chairman*): Thank you, Professor Rees. I do not know whether we should rejoice or be cast down by the knowledge that America is not untroubled by some of these quaint practices. I recently came across a quotation from Robert Lowe, Chancellor of the Exchequer in Gladstone's first government, writing in 1867 in *The Quarterly Review:*
'We do not find fault with the policy of Trades Unions for being selfish; what we object to is that, meaning to be selfish, it is actually suicidal.'
It was some kind of encouragement to know that for a hundred years the same road has been trodden without results that were actually fatal!

STUART BUTLER (*Adam Smith Institute*): I have lived on and off for some time in the United States. In Michigan I came across a railroad operation which was non-union and operating in a very low density area, where the crews were very much smaller than in the union-enforced case: the output per man was much higher and the wage-rates per man were also much higher than union rates. The efficiency and return on capital was also higher than on union railroads. Is this the general case in America? Are we reaching a position with some operators in the United States where, to compete with truckers and so forth, the workers are prepared to work a rather more flexible schedule and to operate in different ways, in return for higher wages, which in turn lead to higher productivity and higher returns for the railroads?

PROF. REES: My general impression is that productivity is higher in non-union establishments than in union establishments in the United States. Obviously there are exceptions, but generally speaking that is so. And in some cases wages are higher in the non-union establishments— that has been particularly true in coal-mining. The Western open-pit coal operators have attracted non-union labour by keeping the total compensation package about the same as in the unionised mines, but they put more of it into the pay envelope and less into fringe benefits, so that take-home pay is higher in the non-union mines. I should add that my casual impressions are contradicted by research recently published in the *Journal of Political Economy*, in which by fitting econometric predictions to American manufacturing, and including variables for the presence or absence of unionisation, the statistical conclusion emerges that productivity is higher in the unionised establishments by enough to offset the wage differential.

I am not a good enough econometrician to criticise econometrics, but I find that a very curious result, because I know no American manufacturing employer who is non-union who does not want to stay that way, and no American manufacturer who is unionised who does not secretly yearn to have the unions go away. Again, there may be a few exceptions but not many. If it is really true that there is a productivity differential that offsets the wage differential, then I am really at a loss to understand why American manufacturing employers are fighting the unions so hard—and many of them are.

BRIAN CHIPLIN (*University of Nottingham*): I would like to ask Professor Rees what he thinks the trade unions are trying to achieve, or, to echo Professor Fisher's question, are they rather irrational or stupid or both? Whichever they are, it seems from the quote we have just heard (from Robert Lowe) to be taking them a long time to find out. How can they get away with it? If we are going to maintain an economy which is open, then if these restrictive practices are not necessary, nor in the workers' interests—and may well not be in the interests even of preserving the jobs of the existing union members—could I have your view on whether unions are in fact doing anyone any good? Does the labour market work, or is it the government—by accommodating expansionary monetary or fiscal policy—that is effectively creating property rights and jobs, which would not otherwise exist?

PROF. REES: I think some of the work-rules are short-sighted and really do result from union members or union leaders not understanding their own best interests. From the point of view of the union member, it is very hard to see the objection to getting rid of over-manning rules through attrition. But it is less hard to understand from the point of view of the union leaders. The union leader is going to be interested in something that preserves the size of his organisation, even conceivably at the expense of the interests of his membership, though obviously he cannot let that conflict become apparent. So there may be some examples of work-rules where 'irrationality' reflects a conflict of interest between leadership and membership.

More generally, American research—there has been extensive research on the size of union/non-union wage differentials, most of it inspired by and much of it carried out by Professor H. Craig Miller at Duke University—consistently shows union/non-union differentials on average of the order of, say, 15 per cent. In some industries like construction it is more like 25 or 30 per cent. And it is not irrational to want to get your relative wage 30 per cent higher than it would otherwise be, particularly if you have a lot of seniority and are therefore assured of continued employment. The costs of this policy in terms of reduced employment are felt by some teenager you do not know who is just trying to enter the labour market. So I would by no means say it is irrational in general for American workers to join unions. The less skilled they are, the bigger the advantage from joining a union, so for unskilled workers to join unions produces a very large increase in their relative wage.

EDGAR PALAMOUNTAIN (*M & G Group*): Professor Phelps Brown contended in a letter to *The Times* recently that if trade unions were to vanish overnight they would simply be re-created by re-grouping under another name. From what Professor Rees was saying, this does not seem to be happening among the non-unionised labour in the United States and I wanted to ask him whether there were any instances where these non-unionised groups of workers were forming bodies which perhaps pursued the positive aims of trade unions but without the restrictionist methods?

W. J. BRIMLEY (*Taylor Woodrow*): I rise in defence of the construction industry in this country. On the Professor's amusing story of the painter in the boat, I would simply say that in this country we work under very strict safety legislation so that it would certainly be a requirement. When my company was carrying out work recently in the Brighton area we would have been severely taken to task if we had not provided those sort of facilities.

Another handicap of the construction industry is that the private sector has often been used as an economic regulator by government, which has prevented us from providing steadier employment and a lot more training opportunities.

The Professor mentioned demarcation several times. I am one who believes that restrictive practices do not create jobs, and if the unions think they do they are utterly mistaken, for restrictive practices simply prolong the operation and raise costs. Demarcation is no longer so prevalent in the construction industry in Britain, but there are still problems. I recall, for example, that when glass bricks were introduced, particularly in the North West, there were half a dozen different unions claiming the exclusive right to handle them because they replaced the work of the painter, the brick-layer, the plasterer, the plumber or the glazier.

My final observation is on job creation. I believe that many employers are deterred from running their businesses efficiently and are deterred from taking on new workers because we now have so much legislation in this country relating to the employment of labour. This legislation is so unfairly weighted in favour of the employee and against the employer that it is detrimental to job creation.

DR JOHN ADDISON: Perhaps the relative wage effect of trade unions is not as you put it, citing Greg Lewis, but closer to the more recent estimates of 3 to 4 per cent, when you allow for the fact that high wages might be a cause of unionism as much as unions causing high wages. One would expect an employer who faces high union wages to seek to improve the quality of his labour, so that union labour is of a higher quality.

PROF. REES: First, on non-union workers forming informal groupings, Professor Phelps Brown is, of course, far more knowledgeable about Great Britain than I am. But I do not think there has been such a tendency recently in the United States. Of course, it is difficult to have a quasi-union in the United States because unionism is governed by the National Labour Relations Act. You are either a certified collective bargaining agent or you are not. We have good records of elections being held for the formation of new unionised bargaining units and unions which used to win about two-thirds are now winning less than half. There are also independent unions, so-called 'company unions' that just cover a particular employer, but I do not see any evidence that they are growing.

On the construction industry, the story of the painter in the boat is not intended to deny the need for a boat or other safety precautions. My main criticism was the requirement that the small rowboat with an outboard motor had to be manned by two people rather than one, and that these men had to be members of the union!

Dr Addison's points are more difficult. When Greg Lewis did his original research, he did not have access to micro-data sets that would enable him to take account of the quality of union labour. So I may very well have quoted a large over-estimate of the true size of the union/non-union wage differential allowing for differing quality. That is, of course, no longer the situation, for we have a number of micro-data sets in the United States that enable us to tell whether the individual worker is or is not a member of a trade union and to provide all of the quality information necessary to construct a Gary Becker/Jacob Menser-type human capital model. My estimate of around 15 per cent is for studies that use a fairly full set of variables on education, race, sex, etc., to adjust for quality. I accept the point that these proxies for quality may be insufficient and that there may be some other quality differentials. For example, John Dunlop is fond of saying that a union craftsman in construction, having served a union apprenticeship, is more skilled than a non-union craftsman and that may very well be true. But I still feel that whatever quality differentials there are in construction cannot be as large as 30 per cent. If they were, I would be totally unable to explain why it is that firms like Brown & Root and Daniels International are expanding so rapidly whereas comparable unionised construction firms are increasingly turning to overseas work.

RALPH HARRIS: Professor Rees, would two minutes allow you to tell us about the picketing laws?

PROF. REES: More than enough, at least to give you the essence of it. The present rule in the construction industry is that if a sub-contractor on a construction site, say an electrical sub-contractor, is engaged in a dispute with the electrical workers' union, and the other contractors on that site do not have a dispute with their workers, then you put up two gates— one for the electrical workers and another for everyone else. The electrical workers' union can only picket their own gate and the other workers go through the second gate. The Common Site Picketing Bill would have allowed the union to picket the entire site.

4 Job 'Creation': Government or Market? West Germany

CHRISTIAN WATRIN

Institute of Economic Policy,
University of Cologne

The Author

CHRISTIAN WATRIN: Professor of Economics, University of Cologne, since 1970. He was formerly Lecturer, University of Cologne, 1963-65; Professor, University of Bochum, 1965-70. He is a member of the Advisory Council to the Federal Ministry of Economics. He has contributed articles for periodicals, and is the author of works (in German) on the principles of the market economy, aspects of social philosophy, Marxism, employment, the economics of apprenticeship and economic development. He is co-editor of an economic journal, *Wirtschaftspolitische Chronik*, and of *ORDO*, an economic and, financial yearbook.

I. INTRODUCTION

Since the 1974-75 recession Germany has had an unemployment problem which gives rise to fierce public debate. Except for the last few months of 1978, the unemployment figures in the official statistics have never fallen short of the one million mark. They have since fallen to 850,000. This result has led to some highly optimistic predictions. The well-known Rheinisch-Westfälische Institut für Wirtschaftsforschung predicts that full employment and monetary stability would be within reach if the trade unions demanded only modest wage increases (a maximum of 3.5 per cent is proposed) and direct taxes were reduced by 5 per cent. Other observers and even government officials are more sceptical.

A more accurate diagnosis of the German unemployment problem indicates that the official figures rather under-estimate the real unemployment rate. Several factors have led to a decrease in the supply of manpower by almost one million since 1974. In addition, half-a-million foreign workers returned to their native countries in southern Europe. Approximately 600,000 people who are not registered as unemployed are looking for jobs, many of them only part-time. Rising birth-rates during the 1960s are now engendering new demands for jobs. Some critics of the official employment policy therefore calculate the 'genuine' number of unemployed as at least two million. But, of course, they do not know the exact amount of voluntary unemployment hidden in the official statistics.

II. GERMANY'S APPROACH TO UNEMPLOYMENT AND INFLATION

Public debate on employment is concentrated on programmes to stimulate the economy and, in particular, to reduce unemployment. A comparison of the subjects being discussed in Germany and abroad leads to the conclusion that German economists are now facing the same politico-economic problems of unemployment and inflation which have been playing an important role elsewhere for a long time. The German inflation rate is, of course, very low by international standards. It fell from 7 to 2.5 per cent during the last three years. But Germans still call this low rate 'inflation'. Germany has had two hyper-inflations during the last 55 years, and the German people are more sensitive to inflation than others. But some popular proposals to fight unemployment and inflation, much discussed in other countries, are not encountered in Germany. There is no large politically influential group laying stress on the doctrine of the 'social contract'. Nor are there—except for some Marxist economists—any adherents of price and wage controls, or any serious advocates of protectionist measures to promote a 'beggar-my-neighbour-policy'.

On current economic problems, there are two main schools of thought. Headed by the Council of Economic Advisers, the first emphasises the importance of wages for the volume of employment and recommends a slight rise in wages combined with a Keynesian programme of modest deficit-spending. The second group demands an active policy of influencing structural and technological changes in the economy, and asks for measures to create jobs with government subsidies, and, most important, to shorten working hours either by law or by industrial agreements.

The German government has acted mainly on the former recommendations, and, since the 1974-75 recession, it has launched more than 10 programmes to stimulate economic activity along these lines. Since it was not very successful—the hope that the economic upswing starting at the beginning of 1976 would gather momentum proved to be too optimistic—a growing number of critics now demands a 'new' policy, especially in the labour market.

German experience in the 1920s
The advocates of the argument that the appropriate employment policy should be based on the redistribution of work and the cutting of working hours are, probably without knowing it, resorting to ideas which, in the name of 'job-creation' and 'relief', had already been tried out in the 1920s and had failed. The political appeal of these proposals cannot be denied. They demand early retirement to provide more vacancies for young people, an extension of holidays (to six weeks), a shorter working week, and the abolition of overtime. It is as though the age of a 'post-industrial leisure time society' is about to dawn. Its advent, apparently, is being prevented only by the small group of economists who continue to preach that resources are scarce, that efficiency is the central economic objective, and that the only way to raise the standard of living is by monetary stability, economic growth and optimal employment.

The advocates of this labour-market 'make-work' policy proceed from the economically untenable assumption that the amount of possible employment does not depend on the price of labour but rather on a given physical quantity of work that can be shared out among the labour force according to the number of jobs, which they seem to think are also fixed quantities. But the supply of and demand for labour are dynamic factors whose reciprocal shifts are guided by the wage-rate. Furthermore, the idea of redistributing the 'amount of work' presupposes that jobs and workers are highly substitutable. In reality, this is not true in an economy with highly specific productive resources.

This proposal does not conform either to the principles of a social market economy or to those of a liberal state. Rules reducing working hours would require rigid controls, including a strict limitation of immigrant labour from the EEC countries.[1] But even a *dirigisme* of the labour market of this kind would not be sufficient. As employment opportunities can be reduced by collective bargaining which leads to settlements that neglect productivity developments, further restrictions on the freedom of employers and unions to settle wage disputes would be unavoidable in the long run.

III. JOB CREATION—PUBLIC AND PRIVATE

More jobs in the 'public sector'

Other groups advocate direct government intervention in the labour market to create jobs by raising the numbers employed in the 'public sector', i.e. by government. During the last 20 years, the total number of government employees has been increasing very rapidly. It is now around 3.5 million, i.e., 16 per cent of the total labour force. The powerful public sector unions have been calling for 300,000 additional jobs.

There are no detailed plans about which 'social needs' should be satisfied by the new government employees. It is always possible to employ people in the sense of giving them a job to do; but the question is whether their work is economically useful. Considerable problems are cropping up here. It is well known that consumers

---

[1] Since 1974 far-reaching restrictions on immigration for citizens of non-member countries of the EEC have been introduced.

cannot express their individual preferences in public goods proper[2] such as defence, so it is impossible to ascertain whether job creation in government leads to the production of economically useful goods. Furthermore, the 'public sector' is not subject to the discipline of the market. Hence, there is more scope for inefficient use of labour.

Doubts must also be expressed about whether a 10 per cent increase in the number of government employees promotes economic expansion. Even if the integration of additional unemployed workers into the economy led to a saving in unemployment insurance, the increase in numbers in government employment would impose considerable costs on the economy in the form of 'invisible' perquisites for civil servants, which are substantial but difficult to quantify, e.g. sickness benefits and generous pensions for which no social insurance contribution has to be paid. There would also be the direct and indirect job costs, for which there are no reliable estimates.

Direct job subsidies
Other proposals envisage direct subsidies for the creation of jobs. Financial aid by the government would be guaranteed once a job has been 'created' and taken up. Or it can be granted as a subsidy to firms for their personnel recruiting costs. When firms take on new staff, they incur considerable costs in advertising, processing the applications, interviewing the applicants, and job training. Hence, the reduction of the 'appointment-cost threshold' is a desirable political measure which, the proponents argue, has the additional advantage of being anti-inflationary because it could be financed by savings in unemployment insurance.

Thus, the main argument in favour of subsidies is that subsidies for the creation of *new* jobs tend to benefit the more dynamic firms. They also avoid the typical mistake of conventional job-creating measures, namely keeping unprofitable enterprises alive by aid from public funds and so contributing to the mis-allocation of scarce resources and draining government funds. This effect has often been proved, particularly in state-owned enterprises.

---

[2] [Goods or services whose consumption by an additional person does not reduce the amount available to others. Individuals who refuse to pay for public goods cannot be excluded from their use, i.e., they gain a 'free ride'. They must therefore be supplied collectively, usually by government. Classic examples include a lighthouse, a television show, and national defence.—ED.]

The argument for subsidies is open to objections. The administrative implementation of providing stimuli for the creation of *new* jobs is difficult. It is impossible to speak of 'work-places' as a given quantity. The dynamic economy, as Schumpeter aptly explained, is characterised by a process of 'creative destruction'—more exactly, 'creative transformation'—which produces not only a constant upheaval of demand and production structures but also of job structures.[3] Hence it may seem that subsidies for the creation of new jobs or the appointment of new employees would benefit the dynamic process. But they may also have complex indirect repercussions on existing jobs. How, for instance, will the transfer within a firm from one work-place to another be managed in a system in which the state subsidises new jobs? German firms frequently try in this way to protect their employees against the consequences of losing their jobs in the dynamic adjustment process. Will the firms then have the right to ask for government subsidies in return for their job-preserving internal policy? If this is so, how strict must government control be in order to avoid fraud and deceit?

Subsidies to new firms also distort existing market competition. Is it not arbitrary to intervene in the freedom of competition by subsidising some but not all competitors? And what are the effects on employment? Is there a substitution of employment opportunities between non-subsidised and subsidised firms? Will the latter provide enough jobs to absorb those people who have lost their jobs with the former?

There have been many such experiments during the last few years. Subsidies were paid not only by the central government but also by local authorities. But there are no detailed evaluations of the efficiency of the whole system. Furthermore, nobody knows the exact amount of taxpayers' money spent, or whether the newly subsidised firms have been operating successfully in the market.

More job-creation subsidies
There were also other job-creating measures introduced under a law to promote working capacity (*Arbeitsförderungsgesetz*). In 1977 the government gave 755 million Deutschmarks (about £189 million) to local authorities and also to some private companies for relief work.

---

[3] Joseph Schumpeter, *Capitalism, Socialism and Democracy*, Unwin University Books, 12th Impression, 1970.

Recipients had to promise not only additional employment but also secure jobs. If they did, the subsidy would be 60 per cent of the direct wages. According to the Council of Economic Advisers, 38,000 jobs were provided. The average cost for the taxpayer thus amounted to 20,000 Deutschmarks (£5,000) per job. The bulk of the money was spent on finding jobs for unemployed clerks, farm workers and personnel in the social services.

In 1977 also the German government paid subsidies to the ship-building, docks, railways, steel, aircraft and textile industries, supposedly to secure jobs. The subsidy to the state-owned railways was approximately 13 billion Deutschmarks (about £3¼ billion), or nearly 6 per cent of the Federal budget. It is difficult to discover the precise amount spent on the other industries. According to the official report on subsidies, published every other year, the total is nearly 15 billion marks. But this represents only the 'visible' monetary value. The innumerable forms of 'invisible' subsidy are not counted, e.g., an extra tax in favour of the coal-mining industry, the so-called 'Kohlepfennig', favourable traffic regulations for railway transport, and protectionist activities such as minimum prices for steel mills in the Common Market.

Improving labour mobility
A further package of measures emphasises the need to reduce the rigidity of the labour market to encourage mobility and improve adjustment to new market conditions. In public discussion, however, proposals of this kind frequently trigger off bitter reactions. A murmur is soon heard that social progress is being undermined. These arguments conceal a sensitive feature of the social security system. Examples are quoted in the press of inflated wage demands by unemployed persons applying for jobs. Conversely, the laws on protection against dismissal and on wage agreements often make it difficult for firms to dismiss their less productive employees and to replace them by better-qualified personnel.

The economic effects of this obstructionist attitude to mobility and flexibility are obvious. Suitable applicants cannot find jobs, and those whose rights of protection against dismissal, which depend on length of service, have a lower priority compared to the 'old timers' are running a greater risk of being dismissed, even if they are more efficient. The total economic costs in inefficiency resulting from reduced mobility cannot be quantitatively assessed, but are probably considerable.

Observers of the labour market thus speak of its division into a primary and a secondary sector. In the primary sector, job risk is small because of the limited possibilities of dismissal. The secondary sector serves as a sort of labour market 'buffer'. Here, the largest group are said to be women and unskilled people, who account for a higher-than-average percentage of the jobless.

This argument is derived from studies in the USA of unemployment among ethnic minorities and the effect of laws of protection against dismissal. The effect of these laws must necessarily be selective, because it is not possible in a dynamic economy to grant everybody uniform protection against dismissal. The stress of competition is thus shifted—exactly as in markets for goods—from the monopolistic to the competitive sectors and here, in addition, it distorts wages.

IV. STIMULUS TO PRIVATE INVESTMENT?

Investment plays a central role in the process of economic growth. Hence, one often hears German public opinion calling for the encouragement of investment, particularly in the private sector, by government as a stimulus to economic activity. For this reason, the Federal Government is considering raising the percentage rates for depreciation (by the diminishing-balance method) to give a stimulus to investment and employment.

This policy raises the basic question of the effects of investment on employment. Here there crops up an old and well-known economic problem which, possibly under the influence of Keynesianism, has been too long neglected. For investment is not only capable of creating employment: in many cases it also raises labour productivity and lays workers off *via* labour-saving inventions. These productivity-increasing and labour-saving effects have recently attracted the attention of the German public. Under the slogan that jobs are 'rationalised away' by investment and hence that unemployment is aggravated, some union leaders have demanded direction of capital investment by local and state boards. These boards should be co-determined, as their proponents argue: half of the seats, for instance, should go to the entrepreneurs, and half to the trade unions. The German phrase for this is '*überbetriebliche Mitbestimmung*'.

85

From the economic point of view, there is a difference between investment-deepening (or capital expenditure on rationalisation) and investment-widening. Investment-deepening leads to an increase in total output of a given labour force by increasing its productivity (or achieving the same output with a smaller labour force); the effect of investment-widening is to increase the labour force without a corresponding increase in productivity, i.e. an investment which increases production but not productivity and therefore creates *new* jobs.

The difference between these two types of investment is theoretical. In reality it is often almost impossible to make a clear distinction. In a dynamic economy, investment normally leads to increased productivity. The same machine is seldom installed after a gap of several years. As history has shown, technical progress and business competition compel industrial firms constantly to keep a sharp look-out for improved investment goods, without this leading to severe unemployment. Nevertheless there are spectacular cases of investment-deepening leading to labour saving. The revolutionising of offices by computerisation or the automation of rolling-mills in steelworks are examples of the possibilities of labour saving by modern large-scale investment.

Investment-deepening . . . or -widening?

It seems proper, therefore, to ask whether it would not, perhaps, be necessary to discourage investment-deepening and to encourage investment-widening, which increases the number of jobs. If such a policy is favoured, several factors must be taken into account.

'Investment-deepening' defines in the first instance only the *motivation* of the entrepreneur when he decides to improve existing production capacity or to supersede it. The economic *effects* can, however, be quite different. When the potential output of the economy as a whole is below full capacity, the effect in the first instance of every new investment—and this includes investment-deepening—is the emergence in the capital goods industry of an additional demand which creates incomes and jobs. The secondary effect of higher incomes, however, can also be seen in the increasing demand for goods in other industries. The effects on employment of investment-deepening are that labour saving in one place is paralleled by job-creation in the capital industries. It would be very difficult to draw up a balance between the two effects on employment, but this argument leads to a simple conclusion: what is labour saving in a single firm need not be so for the economy as a whole.

The evidence

There are some empirical observations to be added to these more theoretical aspects. Between 1970 and 1973, in the Federal Republic of Germany, firms in which rationalisation played a major role employed additional workers because there was an increased demand for their products. Furthermore, it could be observed that investment-deepening (insofar as it can be statistically assessed at all) is, unlike investment-widening, largely independent of the business cycle. On the whole it has a stabilising effect on employment.

There are additional aspects. Any obstacle to investment-deepening would have immediate repercussions on the international competitive power of an economy which relies as heavily on foreign trade as does Germany. Obstacles to investment in rationalisation could trigger off a partial decline in foreign demand for German products, and this in turn would have an adverse effect on employment. But, conversely, in international trade investment-deepening always leads to a stimulation of employment when it succeeds by process- or product-innovation (and this, after all, is what investment-deepening is all about) in improving market prospects. Finally, investment-deepening is the precondition for raising the standard of living. The growth of real wages is possible only to the extent that economic productivity rises.

When the effects on the competitiveness and the welfare of the whole of society are analysed, it is hardly surprising that warnings are constantly being uttered against state intervention in this sector. The Advisory Council to the Federal Ministry of Economics concluded that

'Investment-deepening in a dynamic economy is not only unavoidable but necessary and desirable'

and that

'the hampering or prevention of investment-deepening by *dirigiste* measures, investment controls (including investment registration

87

offices) or prohibitions against rationalisation should be categorically rejected.'[4]

The Council concluded that state economic policy must carefully consider how its decisions affect the relationship between the prices of labour and capital. The sharp rise in wage costs, as a result of the socio-political legislation of the last few years, has undoubtedly had repercussions on employment. Likewise higher percentage rates of depreciation also lower capital costs and, above all, the risk of investing capital. Thus government economic policy should not ignore the influence of such measures on the relation between the prices of capital and labour. In the economic calculation of the firm, this aspect plays an important role in deciding whether investment-deepening is to be undertaken or not.

V. CAN GERMANY RECOVER ITS ECONOMIC DYNAMISM?

Any survey of German economic and, in particular, employment policy raises the questions of whether and to what extent the proposed measures look like being of practical value in mastering the present problem—the recovery of economic dynamism. The required measures include all the means for improving the efficiency of the labour market, particularly those which help to make it less rigid in its adjustment to supply and demand. But such labour-market measures are not enough in themselves to produce an economic upswing. At best they play a supporting role. Germany's main problem today is not so much economic as intellectual and political. The principles of a social market economy are often the subject of heated discussion in public debates. Other systems, like that of a labour-managed socialist economy of the Yugoslav type, enjoy wide esteem. Co-determination between employers and unions/employees in the supervisory boards of the major German concerns is an institutional measure whose economic effects have still to be observed and evaluated.

---

[4] Der Wissenschaftliche Beirat beim Bundesministerium für Wirtschaft (Advisory Council to the Federal Ministry of Economics), *Gutachten vom November 1976 bis November 1977*, Vol. 9, Verlag Otto Schwarz & Co., Göttingen, 1978, p. 848.

It would therefore be naive to assume that, under present conditions, higher depreciation allowances for firms and lower taxes to stimulate consumer demand would be enough to stabilise the upswing.

If the German economy is allowed to recover its dynamism, as a result of social market policies, the many pessimistic prognoses about employment will soon be so much waste paper. For it was the German example of the 1950s and 1960s, when more than 12 million refugees were successfully absorbed into the West German economy, which demonstrated that a market economy whose dynamic potential is encouraged by skilful policy can cope with employment problems which are much more formidable than today's.

5 The Conditions for Labour Productivity—Japan*

YUKIHIDE OKANO
University of Tokyo and
St. Antony's College, Oxford

and

MITSUAKI OKABE
The Bank of Japan

*The views expressed in this paper are those of the authors and not those of the
organisations to which they belong.

The Authors

YUKIHIDE OKANO: Professor of Economics, University of Tokyo since 1976. Formerly Research Associate (Joshu), 1964-66, Associate Professor (Jokyoju), 1966-76, University of Tokyo. Visiting Research Fellow at St Antony's College and Transport Studies Unit, University of Oxford, 1977-79. Author or editor of books on transport economics and policy, public utilities and public economics, including *The Road Haulage Industry in Japan* (1978); *The Economics of Transport* (1977); *Lectures on Transport Economics* (1975); and (with Takashi Negishi as co-editor) *Public Economics* (1973). He has contributed to the Japanese professional periodicals, including *Transportation Studies, Journal of Economics*, and *Quarterly Journal of Economic Studies*. For the IEA he contributed a commentary to *How Japan Competes: A Verdict on 'Dumping'*, by G. C. Allen (Hobart Paper 81, 1978).

MITSUAKI OKABE: graduated from the University of Tokyo in 1968 and joined the Bank of Japan. He studied at the Wharton School, University of Pennsylvania, 1971-73, and gained an MBA. He has been working in the London Office of the Bank of Japan since 1978.

I. INTRODUCTION

It is a well-known theory in economics that demand for labour is a 'derived demand' and therefore depends on the demand for the product it will help to produce and also on the productivity and efficiency of the labour. Thus, it is difficult to see how a 'job creation' programme by government which, by definition, creates something for which there is hardly demand to begin with, can create jobs commensurate with the productivity or efficiency of the labour. We would like to examine the validity of this understanding in the light of the Japanese experience.

Japan's success in raising employment and productivity

Post-war Japanese economic development was very successful in achieving full employment and improving the productivity of labour at the same time. It is generally recognised that when labour productivity increases and other things remain unchanged, the demand for labour decreases so that unemployment increases. If so, Japan must have faced the severest problem of unemployment among the major industrial countries, since Japan has achieved the most conspicuous increase in productivity among them over the past 20 years or so (Table 1). We can cite many contributing factors. Three examples are:

(i) the Japanese ethic that highly regards work itself;

(ii) the strong loyalty of employees to their firm; and

(iii) the stable relationship between workers and employer through the house union system (the loss of working days due to strikes is relatively small) (Table 6).

Contrary to conventional fears that unemployment increases as the productivity of labour increases, the rate of unemployment in Japan has been among the lowest (Table 2). Why, then, has not a rapid increase in productivity entailed severe unemployment in Japan? Has that happy situation changed since the oil crisis because the trend growth rate has been declining? Although Japan has been most successful in slowing down inflation and recovering her balance of trade in a few years, unemployment has been increasing. Are there any problems associated with the Japanese way of dealing with an increase in productivity?[1]

II. PRODUCTIVITY IN JAPAN

1. Productivity and employment during the period of high growth (1958-73)

The 15 years before the oil crisis of 1973 are usually referred to as the high-growth period, or the golden age, for the Japanese economy. The average growth rate was 10.2 per cent per annum, which resulted in a fourfold *real* (not nominal) growth of GNP. During this stage, the achievement of rapid productivity increase was the cause as well as the effect of high growth; and the negative impact of increased productivity on employment virtually did not appear at all.

To explain this phenomenon, we must examine the relationship between growth rate and productivity. In the circumstances of growing world trade, and especially of United States imports, and helped by the fixed-exchange-rate régime, exports grew rapidly (at an average of 14.1 per cent per annum) (Table 3). This growth directly increased industrial production and GNP, which in turn induced private investment in plant and equipment. The investment was further accelerated by the necessity of catching-up with innovations in advanced countries and of competing with their products in overseas markets. Since investment raised the capital-labour ratio, the result was naturally a rapid increase in labour productivity, and an improvement in international competitiveness.

These circumstances gave still further impetus to the increase in exports and production in the second stage. In this process, the real wage-rate in manufacturing rose by 8 per cent per annum on average between 1963 and 1973, which helped the growth of personal consumption expenditure, and hence the GNP. This period may be characterised as the high-growth period led chiefly by exports and

---

[1] Productivity in general refers to the ratio of output to one of the factors of production, hence productivity of labour, productivity of capital and that of input of raw materials, etc., of which we concentrate on the productivity of labour (real output per employee) since this has the greatest implication for the labour market. And our attention will be focussed solely on productivity in manufacturing industry, except as otherwise mentioned, since it is relatively easy to quantify and to make international comparisons.

brisk private investment, and we can say, in a sense, that the economy was enjoying a 'virtuous circle'.

Surprisingly this rapid productivity rise caused no problems in the labour market. This was because the expansion of aggregate demand, from overseas as well as from domestic sources, was so rapid in terms of GNP that the labour force for the increased requirement of production was absorbed without any slack developing. Indeed, the gain in productivity was not sufficient to meet the combined growth in demand for production so that the labour market simply became *tighter*[2] (Table 4). In this situation, the increase in productivity obviously causes no adverse effect on the labour market. And labour was allocated to industries where production was increasing most rapidly. It was through this market process of labour allocation that Japan has successfully transformed its backward industrial structure into an 'advanced' one, by eventually eliminating inefficient and less productive industries[3] (Table 5).

2. Productivity and employment after the oil crisis (1973-present)

After the oil crisis the picture changed because the growth rate fell sharply from 10.2 to 4.2 per cent (Table 3). The quadrupling of oil prices, coupled with the prevalence of general uncertainty, made business firms reduce their expectations of medium-term growth. It cut down aggregate private investment (through the acceleration principle working in the opposite direction), that is, the anticipation of a low rate of increase in future output markedly reduced private investment, which in turn brought about a deflationary pressure on aggregate demand. On the other hand, exports, which increased even faster after the oil crisis, could not now be expected to continue to grow as fast, not only because of the rapid appreciation of the yen, but also because of increasingly severe criticism (hostility?) from overseas of the rapid growth of Japanese exports. Consequently, the

---

[2] The increase in junior and senior high school graduates who followed advanced courses during this period helped the labour market become tighter. The participation rate of youths aged between 15 and 19 fell from 38.6% in 1965 to 23.0% in 1975.

[3] Probably the coal-mining industry in the early 1960s was the notable exception in which extensive government support was required to re-allocate a considerable number of workers from the depressed coal-mining industry to other industries. Employment in coal-mining fell from 413,000 in 1952 to 212,000 in 1961 and to 34,000 in 1972.

lack of vitality in these two leading demand components implied inevitably a decline in the growth rate. In other words, the chain of the virtuous circle in aggregate demand broke down.

On the other hand, the pressure on business firms to increase productivity has not weakened but become stronger. This is, first, because of the rapid price increase of input raw materials, notably of oil prices, and, secondly, because of continually rising wage-rates. To prevent profits from diminishing under these circumstances, business strategy has been compelled to give productivity increase a continued high priority. In addition, the rapid and continual appreciation of the yen has further compelled firms to increase productivity, although it was partly offset by the decline in the yen prices of imported materials.

Thus, the decline in the growth of aggregate demand and the increased pressure for raising productivity have led businesses to reconsider the size of their labour force, which had been expanded on the assumption that the high growth would be maintained rather than being abruptly interrupted after the oil crisis. In this way, labour difficulties in Japan emerged as a serious problem of fundamentally the same nature as in European slow-growth economies. The performance of the Japanese economy in this respect seems so far comparatively good.

After the oil crisis, the productivity rise of 3.5 per cent per annum was internationally one of the highest and was achieved by drastic reduction in the employed labour force (Table 1). As had been expected, slack suddenly developed in the labour market, and in 1977 there were nearly twice as many job applications as unfilled vacancies, while in the previous period of a tighter labour market unfilled job vacancies were nearly twice as high as job applications (Table 4). Even in this situation, however, unemployment is still at the low rate of 2 per cent (though unemployment is narrowly defined in Japan in comparison with other countries). How has it been possible?

3. The Japanese mechanism of labour-force adjustment
What must be emphasised here is that the basic mechanism which has worked since the oil crisis is fundamentally the same as that during the high-growth era, although the differing economic situations have brought about widely different results. We will first take up the managerial aspect of labour within a business firm and then its

market aspect, to explain why the Japanese system has worked so well.

(i) Labour management within a firm
The first key is that of labour management within a firm; that is, the allocation and re-allocation of labour from one plant to another or from one region to another, which has been achieved quite flexibly within a firm or group of firms. In the high-growth period, all or some of the labour force of an old plant was re-allocated to newly-built plant where productivity was highest.[4] Even after the oil crisis this kind of labour adjustment played an important role.

In cutting the excessive labour force to an optimal amount or composition, for example, firms tried not only to reduce the number of new employees but also to make the best use of such methods as the temporary placement of workers in other businesses, typically in subsidiaries, and re-allocation within a firm. And most managements usually preferred these measures to the more drastic dismissal or voluntary resignation (Figure 1). To give a concrete example, IHI (Ishikawajima-Harima Heavy Industry), a giant shipbuilding and machinery firm, decided to reduce the labour force in its shipyards by shifting workers to plants where general machinery is produced. Moreover, since such a transfer of workers alone was not sufficient to eliminate excess labour within the firm, IHI is reported to have temporarily placed as many as 2,500 of its workers with Toshiba, with which it has close connections and which required additional labour.

Isuzu Motor, which has absorbed more than 1,200 workers from steel and non-ferrous metal companies, is an example of the advantages of this kind of measure. First, the workers are well-trained and very productive; secondly, the cost of recruitment of employees can be saved; and, thirdly, no considerable adjustment of employment would be required even if the company was obliged to decrease its production. Nippon Steel, on the other hand, which has sent these workers to Isuzu Motor, also illustrates the advantage that it can

---

[4] Re-allocation of labour force includes the geographical. A notable example was that Hitachi, the largest manufacturers of electrical appliances and electronics in Japan, closed one of its biggest plants in Tokyo and re-allocated all the workers to newly-built plants in other areas.

Figure 1: Changes in Employment Adjustment Methods: Japan (All Industries)

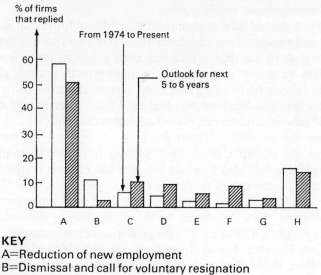

KEY
A=Reduction of new employment
B=Dismissal and call for voluntary resignation
C=Placements with subsidiaries
D=Re-location within a business firm
E=Restriction on wage rise
F=Re-structuring of wage rate
G=Others
H=No adjustment necessary

Source: Economic Planning Agency, *Economic Survey of Japan, 1977-78.*

save personnel costs even if it makes up the difference in wages between them.[5]

Fairly extensive internal allocation and relocation of labour are initiated by business firms at managerial discretion. Thus, labour management within a firm partially plays the role of the labour market itself. Even if the labour market does not appear efficient or flexible (because, for example, of 'life-time employment'), the *intra*-firm re-allocation of labour results in *inter*-industry, *inter*-regional re-allocation of labour, thus making the allocation of labour as a whole efficient. This is one of the important aspects of the Japanese mechanism that has achieved a remarkable increase in productivity

---

[5] *Nihon Keizai Shinbun*, 5 October 1978.

while keeping unemployment low. It has also helped make the social problem of unemployment less serious, which, in turn, has reduced the frequency and length of labour disputes (Table 6), while further helping productivity to increase.

Two basic conditions favour the working of this mechanism. The first is the willingness of workers to take up different kinds of jobs, even if they are unfamiliar with them or in a geographically remote region. This readiness to change jobs and homes stems from the Japanese promotion system in which workers are usually promoted not to the higher levels of the same job but rather to the higher levels of different but similar jobs within a plant, or at a different, sometimes remote, plant.

The second condition is the entrepreneurship of business managers in both the offensive and defensive sense, together with the competitive environment that compels them to remain so. It is only when competition prevails and business profit is threatened with decline that a firm will take the stern measures described to adjust its labour force and cut labour costs to a minimum.

(ii) Labour market forces
The second key to high productivity concerns the effectiveness of market forces in general in allocating and re-allocating labour. The labour market in Japan may be said to play the role of adjusting only marginal labour, such as new school leavers, temporary workers and 'drop-outs' from firms. It is of secondary importance only because it lacks scope and size where the main body of workers is employed by businesses under life tenure. What matters is the market, or competitive pressure, throughout the whole economy.

Our description of *intra*-firm mobility of labour, backed finally by market forces, mainly affects larger firms. In smaller firms, the adjustment depends on the intensity of a fiercer battle for survival; inefficient firms are forced to release their labour to be absorbed by other, more productive firms. The statistics of corporate bankruptcies show that, after the oil crisis, the number rose from between 10,000 and 13,000 to above 18,000 in 1977 (Table 7). Apart from cyclical factors, this can be interpreted as implying that the change in industrial structure and re-allocation of labour has been taking place under slower economic growth, and that it is one of the symptoms of an economy that remains competitive and healthy.

Another remarkable example may be the change in the number of employees in the shipbuilding industry, now depressed worldwide. In the previous most prosperous period, the total number of employees of the 23 main shipbuilders, all private firms, was over 113,000 in October 1974, compared with 90,000 in April 1978. Thus, as many as 23,000, or 20 per cent of all such employees, have left shipbuilding during the short period of 3½ years.[6] This reduction was achieved through intra-firm and inter-firm re-allocation of labour, as well as through redundancies brought about by bankruptcies. Such a rapid and drastic reduction of the number of employees would not have been possible without this re-allocation mechanism, or if shipbuilding firms had been public corporations.[7]

III. PROBLEMS OF STRUCTURAL UNEMPLOYMENT

The inevitable increase in unemployment following this process causes problems in three ways.

'Structural', age-group and 'hidden' unemployment

First, most unemployment is 'structural' unemployment in distressed industries and cannot easily be moved into other industries. Textiles, aluminium refining, shipbuilding and the iron and steel industries are the typical examples, though the reasons for their distress differ. Some have lost international competitiveness because of the industrial progress in developing countries, the high price of energy, and the appreciation of the yen. Some also suffer from excess production capacities because of the worldwide decline in demand and/or restrictions on exports by importing countries. Also, with low economic growth and hostility to Japanese exports, industries such as motor-cars and electronics cannot give many job opportunities to the unemployed. Thus, re-allocation of labour cannot be as smooth as previously.

---

[6] The Japan Shipbuilders Association agreed to the proposal by the Shipping and Shipbuilding Rationalisation Council, Department of Transportation, to scrap 35 per cent of shipbuilding capacity.

[7] Compared with private firms, it is extremely hard for public enterprises to adopt such re-allocation measures. Labour disputes in the transport and communications industries, in which most employees are those of public enterprises, such as Japanese National Railways and Nippon Telephone and Telegraph Public Corporation, account for some 20-30 per cent of the total (Table 6).

Figure 2: Labour Market situation by Age Groups: Japan, 1976

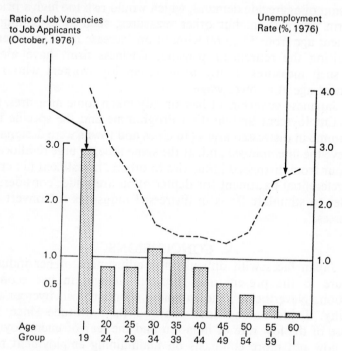

Source: Economic Planning Agency, *Economic Survey of Japan, 1976-77.*

Second, the impact tends to be felt unevenly by differing age groups (Figure 2). The older workers have more difficulty in finding jobs because the seniority-based wage system makes firms naturally prefer to employ younger workers. Thus workers over 55 are suffering most since, even though the prevailing retirement age is 55, the majority feel obliged to work to maintain their incomes.

Third, there has clearly been widespread 'hidden unemployment'. The most common example takes the form of housewives withdrawing from the labour market when unable to find jobs—what economists describe as a fall in the 'participation rate'. Again, college graduates tend to take up jobs such as postmen, for which they are over-qualified. Such results of downward adjustment in demand for labour may squeeze the job opportunities for young school-leavers.

Towards solutions

The solution to this 'structural' problem is not, in our opinion, the expansion of aggregate demand, which would risk too high a price in the form of inflation, but other measures, such as extending the retirement age from 55 to 60 without an increase in wages after 55, and raising the retirement pension. Business firms have already taken such measures. Many firms re-employ workers who reach retirement age at a lower wage.

The Japanese government has already taken some measures, such as the Employment Stabilisation Programme and the specific relief programme in distressed areas (16 cities and towns were designated), to relieve the unemployed and, at the same time, to urge re-allocation of labour from distressed industries to others. Investment tax credits and preferential treatment for depreciation are under consideration in order to stimulate firms in distressed industries to convert their businesses.

IV. CONCLUSIONS

Thus, Japan faces with difficulty the adjustment of her industrial structure to the present and foreseen changes in her economic condition. Nevertheless, the Japanese economy will overcome the difficulty. Trade unions have changed their attitude since 1978, because of the low rate of inflation and the fear of unemployment. They now put more emphasis on maintaining employment rather than wage increases in the so-called 'spring offensive'—the spring wage bargaining season. The trade unions of profitable companies refrained from claiming large increases in wages, taking account of the hardship of workers in the distressed industries. Some trade unions of companies in the distressed industries went even further and accepted wage cuts to maintain employment as far as possible. Wage cuts of general workers used to be preceded by cuts in salary of senior staffs. Thus, trade unions and managers are said to be trying to solve the problems in co-operation with each other. However, the managers of a few successful companies in the distressed industries criticise managers who are obliged to dismiss employees or cut wages on the ground that really good managers should be able to do without such measures. As long as such vigour of management continues, the present difficulty will be overcome.

In these circumstances, the unemployment relief of the Japanese government will not go so far as to have an adverse effect on the incentive to work. There is strong opposition among the Japanese against 'too much dole'.

Postscript

This paper was written in November 1978. No textual revisions have been made and the authors believe that what they wrote is still true; but three observations should be added on the intervening period.

First, Japan's seasonally adjusted unemployment rate fell rapidly to 2.06 per cent in February 1979 after reaching its peak of 2.3 per cent in November 1978, when it was anticipated that it would continue to rise in early 1979. This fall in unemployment is attributable to the recovery of the Japanese economy during 1978. It should be noted that the employment of female workers increased and that their 'participation rate', which fell drastically during the depression of 1974-75, has also risen again since 1977. But unemployment among middle-aged and older male workers has been increasing steadily. The unemployment of male workers as a whole in January 1979 was lower by 20,000 compared with January 1978, but the number of unemployed male workers over 40 increased by 60,000 in the year.

Second, the government has appropriated 1,734,000 million yen (about £3,853 million), 14.4 per cent more than in the 1978 fiscal year, for the employment stabilisation measures in the budget for the 1979 fiscal year, in order to relieve unemployment, particularly among older workers, whose employment stabilisation grant was given priority. A notable example is the government grant to employers who increase employment of workers over 55. The grant covers four-fifths of the wages of newly-employed older workers.

Third, it has been said by some economists, commentators and even corporate managers that the traditional Japanese employment system, which is characterised by life-time employment and seniority wage-payment, will break down because of the recent reductions in employment by depressed industries. Our view is that the Japanese employment system will not break down, though it may be modified to some extent. Managers of firms will not change long-lived employment practices drastically, because they are careful not to impair the incentive of workers to work based on traditions which are, in general, accepted by the workers.

Job 'Creation'—or Destruction?

Statistical Appendix to Paper 5

TABLE 1

PRODUCTIVITY, EMPLOYMENT AND OUTPUT IN
MANUFACTURING: SELECTED COUNTRIES,
1960-73 TO 1973-77

Trend rate of growth per cent per annum

		1960-73	1973-77
		%	%
JAPAN	Productivity	8.8	3.5
	Employment	3.1	—2.9
	Output	12.0	0.5
W. GERMANY	Productivity	5.0	3.6
	Employment	0.3	—3.3
	Output	5.3	0.4
UNITED STATES	Productivity	3.4	2.7
	Employment	1.5	—1.1
	Output	4.9	1.6
FRANCE	Productivity	5.6	2.0
	Employment	0.3	—1.1
	Output	5.9	0.9
UNITED KINGDOM	Productivity	3.4	0
	Employment	—0.4	—1.8
	Output	3.0	—1.8

Source: Bank of England *Quarterly Bulletin*, September 1978, p. 340.

TABLE 2

COMPARISON OF UNEMPLOYMENT RATES:
SELECTED COUNTRIES, 1970 AND 1977

	Japan	USA	UK	W. Germany	Italy
	%	%	%	%	%
1970	1.2	4.9	2.5	0.7	3.1
1977	2.0	7.0	6.1	4.5	7.2

Note: Figures for the USA and Italy include the temporarily laid-off.
In Japan the definition of unemployment for statistical purposes is
restrictive, so that the figures appear artificially lower than those of
other countries.

Source: Bank of Japan, *Statistics of International Comparisons*, 1978.

TABLE 3
GROWTH IN REAL GNP, PRIVATE INVESTMENT IN PLANT AND EQUIPMENT, AND EXPORTS: JAPAN, 1958-73 TO 1973-77

	1958-1973 (fiscal years) per cent per annum %	*1973-1977 (fiscal years)* per cent per annum %
Real GNP	10.2	4.2
of which:		
Private investment in plant and equipment	15.7	—2.5
Private consumption	8.7	5.5
Exports	14.1	14.9

Source: Calculated from National Income Statistics by the Japanese Economic Planning Agency.

TABLE 4
LABOUR PRODUCTIVITY AND LABOUR MARKET SITUATION: JAPAN, 1963 TO 1977

	Labour Productivity Index: Manufacturing (1970 Average=100)		*Ratio of Job Vacancies to Job Applicants*
	Index	% Increase	
1963	45.9	9.8	0.70
1964	51.5	12.2	0.80
1965	53.3	3.5	0.64
1966	60.2	12.9	0.74
1967	70.2	16.6	1.00
1968	79.8	13.7	1.12
1969	90.6	13.5	1.30
1970	100.0	10.4	1.41
1971	104.4	4.4	1.12
1972	116.0	11.1	1.16
1973	139.3	20.1	1.76
1974	140.4	0.8	1.20
1975	133.3	—5.1	0.61
1976	151.4	13.6	0.64
1977	159.1	5.1	0.56

Source: Japanese Productivity Centre and Ministry of Labour.

TABLE 5

COMPOSITION OF MANUFACTURING PRODUCTION: JAPAN, 1958, 1963 AND 1973

	1958 %	1963 %	1973 %
Total Manufacturing Production	100	100	100
of which:			
'Light' industries	53	38	32
'Heavy' industries	47	62	68

Note: 'Light' industries include fibres, glass-ceramics, food, lumber and wood products, pulp-paper.
'Heavy' industries include iron and steel, non-ferrous metals, fabricated metals, machinery, chemicals and petroleum.

Source: Calculated from manufacturing indexes by Ministry of International Trade and Industry.

TABLE 6

LABOUR DISPUTES IN ALL INDUSTRIES (INCLUDING PUBLIC CORPORATIONS): SELECTED COUNTRIES, 1968 TO 1976

		Participants in strikes ('000)	Days lost ('000 days)	Of which transport and communications industries ('000)	('000 days)
Japan	1968	1,163	2,841	248	639
	1969	1,412	3,634	415	1,037
	1970	1,720	3,915	403	819
	1971	1,896	6,029	443	1,250
	1972	1,544	5,147	443	2,000
	1973	2,236	4,604	628	1,252
	1974	3,621	9,663	1,053	2,721
	1975	2,732	8,016	931	2,441
	1976	1,356	3,254	448	1,274

TABLE 6 (continued)

		Participants in strikes	*Days lost*	*Of which transport and communications industries*
United States	1968	2,649	49,018	
	1969	2,481	42,869	
	1970	3,305	66,414	
	1971	3,280	47,589	
	1972	1,714	27,066	
	1973	2,251	27,948	
	1974	2,778	47,991	
	1975	1,746	31,237	
	1976	2,420	37,859	
United Kingdom	1968	2,255	4,690	
	1969	1,654	6,846	
	1970	1,793	10,980	
	1971	1,171	13,551	
	1972	1,722	23,909	
	1973	1,513	7,197	
	1974	1,622	14,750	
	1975	789	6,012	
	1976	666	3,284	
West Germany	1968	25	25	
	1969	90	249	
	1970	184	93	
	1971	334	2,599	
	1972	23	66	
	1973	185	563	
	1974	250	1,051	
	1975	36	69	
	1976	169	534	

TABLE 6 (continued)

		Participants in strikes	Days lost	Of which transport and communications industries
France	1968	464	423	
	1969	1,444	2,224	
	1970	1,080	1,742	
	1971	3,235	4,388	
	1972	2,721	3,755	
	1973	2,246	3,915	
	1974	1,564	3,380	
	1975	1,827	3,869	
	1976	3,814	5,011	
Italy	1968	4,862	73,918*	
	1969	7,507	302,597	
	1970	3,722	146,212	
	1971	3,891	103,590	
	1972	4,405	136,480	
	1973	6,133	163,935	
	1974	7,824	136,267	
	1975	14,110	190,324	
	1976	11,898	177,643	

*Hours lost.
Source: As for Table 2.

TABLE 7

CORPORATE BANKRUPTCIES:
JAPAN, 1965 TO 1977
(*Number*)

1965	10,152
1967	13,683
1969	10,658
1971	11,489
1973	10,862
1974	13,605
1975	14,477
1976	16.842
1977	18,741

Note: Figures indicate the number of suspensions of business transactions with banks (for corporations with capital of 1 million yen or more).
Source: Federation of Bankers' Association of Japan.

Questions and Discussion

RALPH HARRIS (*Chairman*): We have had an exposition of the differing approaches to unemployment from countries with contrasting political, philosophical, and social environments. The question is whether there are any lessons we can learn in Britain.

STANLEY SEIBERT (*University of Stirling*): I would like to ask Professor Okano to expand a little on the Japanese government's legislation on the labour market. In particular, do you have any redundancy payments legislation, dismissals legislation, and so on? Could you also expand a little on your comment about the level of unemployment benefit? What proportion is it of the average wage?

PROF. PETER SLOANE (*Paisley College of Technology*): I was interested in Professor Watrin's comments about the relative prices of capital and labour which I think is relevant to a number of countries. Earlier today disparaging comments were made about the theory of the second best. But it is quite true to say that through regional policies there has been an implicit subsidy to capital; in the UK the subsidy is equivalent to 22 per cent. It seems to me it would be far more sensible, without any additional cost to the Exchequer, to have 11 per cent subsidy to capital and 11 per cent to labour. The only argument against that would be that one believes capital-intensive investment in some way stimulates a higher rate of economic growth. I have not seen any evidence to suggest that is so.

Extremely topical, too, is the question of work-sharing which the unions seem to think is the answer to problems of unemployment. Basically, of course, this depends on whether unions are prepared to accept a reduction in the *weekly* wage, in other words that hourly wage-rates remain the same, but fewer hours are worked per man. I suspect there is a reluctance to accept that as the situation. One of the main features in the post-war period in virtually all the OECD countries is the remarkable increase in the ratio of non-wage to wage costs. In some cases the ratio is 70 per cent, i.e. non-wage costs are 70 per cent of wage costs. This increase in the fixed costs of labour means that employers' attempts to minimise costs will be concentrated on using their existing labour force more intensively rather than taking on extra labour. If we accept that there is a case for subsidisation, governments really ought to think about reducing non-wage costs and, therefore, it appears that governments which increase national insurance contributions are not really helping to stimulate employment.

ROBERT JACKSON (*Candidate for European Parliament*): This question is really for Professor Okano. This morning there was a lot of adverse comment on the economics of state intervention to create or maintain jobs.

I was very interested in his rather positive account of action by firms in Japan to maintain or create jobs. I wonder if he could comment on the economics of Japan as compared with the discussion this morning?

PROF. MALCOLM R. FISHER: I would like to make a further request for elucidation from Professor Okano. Is the shifting of labour from one firm to another done in a lump or is it spread over time? Secondly, on the supply side, is there something particularly versatile about the Japanese skilled worker whereby his skills are more adaptable than in this and other countries?

PROF. OKANO: On the first question about unemployment, if my memory is correct, the benefit depends on how long a man is employed and how much he pays for unemployment insurance. I think a worker employed for several years will get something like 50-60 per cent of his wage. But I think the period of unemployment compensation is much shorter than in the UK.

There are two or three ways of unemployment compensation. A small business relies heavily on government unemployment compensation. The employees of a small enterprise will get less than the big enterprise where the employees have unemployment compensation paid not only by the government but also by the company.

I must say something about non-state job creation through the market. It will be easier if I stick to the Japanese labour market. There are many examples, such as the employees of IHI shifting to Toshiba; another is that one of the biggest building companies, Mitsubishi, moves some workers from heavy industry into the Mitsubishi motor company and some to Mitsubishi motor sales company. So some clerks in the building company will become salesmen in the Mitsubishi motor company. Of course, the Mitsubishi heavy industry company selects those who are best fitted to be salesmen. In that way those who would otherwise be unemployed will be re-deployed more by the company than by government intervention.

ROBERT JACKSON: Why does it work with private industry and not with the state. Is it because the firms are wiser?

PROF. OKANO: The Japanese companies, particularly big companies, have their own system of education—the Toyota Motor Company even has a senior high school near the plant. Through their education system, managers know who is not good for this or that kind of job; also the kind of training makes it easy to switch to new requirements. I have an example taken from a newspaper report: the case of Isuzu Motor Company, now a joint venture with General Motors. Each had to absorb more than 1,200 workers from steel and non-ferrous companies, and there are several advantages. First, the workers who are sent by the bigger enterprises are well trained and very productive. Second, the cost of recruitment of employees can be saved. Third, no considerable adjustment to employment would be required even if the company was obliged to increase production.

On the other hand, the steel industry, which has sent workers to Nippon Motors, also points to the advantage that it can reduce its wage costs even if it has to make up the difference of wages between them. From the viewpoint of the economy as a whole, this kind of re-allocation of labour is much more efficient.

RALPH HARRIS: If I may abuse my role in the chair, I would suggest to Dr Jackson that whether or not in his words entrepreneurs are wiser than governments in intervention, politicians will often, despite the rhetoric, be concerned with very short-term, even fleeting advantages to get them round the next corner. Entrepreneurs are almost certainly bound to take a longer view and within the limited options that are available to try and take steps that will preserve the enterprise into the future. We have heard that a week is the time-horizon in politics. That seems an important distinction.

PROF. WATRIN: On Mr Sloane's question, may I say that the capital and labour relationship is very important for every firm. Germany is now a high labour-cost country which leads to German firms investing in the United States where labour costs are often lower. If you analyse wage costs in terms of direct and indirect wage costs, the normal situation is that if a worker's salary goes up by 10 marks he has a deduction of about 6 marks for taxes and social insurance. This has important economic side-effects—in Germany you can watch a black market developing and flourishing. On Saturdays you can get bricklayers, carpenters, and other craftsmen much more cheaply than the regular firms which operate from Monday to Friday. These are all the result of our very high labour costs.

MARTIN WASSELL (*International Chamber of Commerce*): I am curious to know how this intra-company and indeed inter-company allocation system seems to work so smoothly in Japan, particularly when it involves apparent immobility between regions. Apart from the obvious penalties and incentives in maintaining or losing a job, are other additional penalties and incentives built in? For example, does the company help with mobility grants? Does it provide new company housing? And similarly on the penalty side, does a man who refuses to move when offered a job lose company housing? Does he find that he does not have the same full employment benefit as perhaps someone who is declared redundant and is not able to do anything to prevent it?

PROF. OKANO: As soon as an employee is shifted to a remote area, he will be provided with a company house. Also I believe that if some employees do not wish to go to a remote area and refuse to move, they will be disadvantaged in promotion.

NOEL PICARDA-KEMP (*Union of Independent Companies and Prospective Conservative Candidate for Lewisham West*): I would like to ask Professor Okano what proportion of housing is company owned and whether there is substantial state intervention or municipal intervention in the housing market in Japan? And how do you achieve flexibility of housing when moving workers? One of our problems in Britain is that we have housing 'serfs' who are tied to their council houses at low rents and therefore do not want to move.

PROF. OKANO: We have housing difficulties, too, especially in big cities like Tokyo. That is why companies provide their employees with homes. If the housing market works smoothly the workers find houses by themselves. Housing corporations provide some houses but it is not a big share. Generally speaking, it is easy to move from the big cities to the countryside to find a house or other accommodation, but it is very hard the other way—to get houses in the big cities. So in practice Japanese companies play the role of government in this country, I should say.

RICHARD HENDERSON (*Sheppards & Chase*): One of the clearest indications, at a purely anecdotal level, of the distortions in the UK labour market is the great strength of the so-called 'do-it-yourself' movement, whereby it is much cheaper in terms of direct costs to do virtually anything inefficiently oneself than to go through the labour market and have the thing done efficiently by someone else. Given that we have an unusually distorted labour market, one would expect that such do-it-yourself movements would be much smaller in many other countries. Is that the experience of our speakers today?

PROF. OKANO: The do-it-yourself movement is not very popular in Japan, except for fun or recreation.

PROF. WATRIN: Do-it-yourself is very popular in Germany but I do not know of any serious study in which people have been asked whether it is for fun or to save expense. If you employ a carpenter or similar craftsman at the normal rate through a firm you have to pay him 35 marks per hour. If you employ him personally on Saturdays, you pay only 10 or 12 marks, only one-third of the rate, and it is very easy to get people on Saturdays to do carpentry or anything else.

RALPH HARRIS: That is in cash, of course?

PROF. WATRIN: Yes. The black market is very well developed!

CHRISTOPHER MEAKIN (*CBI*): Since we have both German and Japanese experts with us, it seems an opportune moment, talking about labour productivity, to try out one of the pet theories of British politicians at present, which is that every economy has somewhere in its system a hidden sink of unemployment. The sad thing about the British economy is that whereas its agriculture and retail distribution system are comparatively efficient, its manufacturing industry is chronically inefficient. The comparison has been drawn with West Germany and France which by comparison have efficient productive industries and inefficient agriculture. They have their hidden sink of unemployment in their agricultural sector.

It is alleged that in the Japanese economy they have very efficient productive industries but that their retail distribution sectors are positively Byzantine and that that is their sink of unemployment. Of course it makes life doubly difficult for an inefficient British producer trying to export into an inefficient Japanese distributive system, whereas the lucky, efficient Japanese manufacturer enjoys all the benefits of an extremely efficient British retail and distributive system.

PROF. OKANO: It is true that in former days hidden unemployment was found in agriculture.

In Japanese retailing the requirements of the consumer are different from here. Thus, 90 per cent of all Japanese newspapers are delivered to the door every day; and when a newspaper wanted to abandon its delivery service the Japanese consumers objected, even if they had to pay more for the service. The Japanese consumer thinks that everything he buys should be delivered to his home as quickly as possible. That is what makes the retail and distributive industries in Japan inefficient from the viewpoint of Western people.

PROF. WATRIN: I do not think there is much hidden unemployment in Germany. I have a figure for employment in agriculture, it is 6.6 per cent of the whole work force—not very much.

RALPH HARRIS: I am going to thank Professor Watrin and our two Japanese speakers, Professor Okano and Mr Okabe, for their performance which, conducted by them in a foreign language, puts most of us to shame. I ask you to express your gratitude. (*Applause.*)

113

6 Public Policy

WALTER ELTIS

University of Oxford

The Author

WALTER ELTIS: Fellow of Exeter College and Lecturer in Economics, University of Oxford, since 1963. He was Visiting Reader in Economics at the University of Western Australia, 1970 and Visiting Professor of Economics, University of Toronto, 1976-77. He has been a general editor of *Oxford Economic Papers* since 1974 and he was an Economic Consultant to the National Economic Development Office from 1963 until 1966. Since 1977 he has been Economic and Financial Consultant to Rowe and Pitman. He is the author of *Growth and Distribution* (1973); co-author with Robert Bacon of *Britain's Economic Problem: Too Few Producers* (1976); joint editor of *Induction Growth and Trade* (1970); and he has published articles on Adam Smith and François Quesnay. For the IEA, with Robert Bacon, he contributed 'How Growth in Public Expenditure has Contributed to Britain's Difficulties', in *The Dilemmas of Government Expenditure* (Readings 15, 1976).

One of the more helpful features of the papers at this Seminar has been the way in which a number of fashionable palliatives have been attacked and, one would hope, disposed of. Dr Addison has been most helpful in explaining how little is to be expected from job subsidies and the dangers in extensive job creation in the public services. Professor Fisher has echoed this criticism and explained from a new angle how little is to be hoped for from ordinary Keynesian policies because they rest fundamentally on persuading workers to accept a lower real wage than they would otherwise wish to accept. As soon as workers realise that it is a lower real wage that is raising employment, they react by attempting to raise money wages more rapidly, and the economy returns to the former volume of unemployment at a much higher level of prices than before. There were, more hopefully, indications to the answers to the employment problem from the papers of our visitors from West Germany and Japan. In particular, when Professor Watrin said that there had been a Schumpeterian process of 'creative destruction' in West Germany he was emphasising the necessity for the destruction of bad and unprofitable jobs as part of the process by which profitable new ones are created. The same appeared to be true of Japan.

British employment trends
Some of the basic British employment statistics are set out in Table 1 so that the size of the problem that Britain faces can be assessed. For the period 1977-87 we extrapolate the trend of 1966-73, the period immediately preceding the world recession, to show where we will get to if it continues.

What is really disturbing about the British employment trends set out in the Table—and they have disturbed many—is the fall of 1,916,000 in employment in industry from 1966 to 1976. And note that of this fall 1,087,000 occurred before the world recession. So we were running into trouble in Britain well *before* the start of the world recession. The private service sector together with the self-employed created 1,113,000 new jobs from 1966 to 1977; but, on balance, industry, agriculture and the private services, that is, the full market sector of the economy, lost 1,090,000 jobs from 1966 to 1977, and it dropped 625,000 before the world recession.

Job 'Creation'—or Destruction?

TABLE 1

BRITISH EMPLOYMENT TRENDS, 1966-1977,
WITH PROJECTIONS TO 1987
(*Thousands*)

	1966	1973	1976	1977	(1987)
Labour force	25,066	25,545	26,136	26,367	(27,388)
Market sector employment	20,707	20,082	19,467	19,617	(18,832)
of which:					
Industry	11,002	9,915	9,086	9,153	
Agriculture	565	434	382	381	
Transport and communications	1,598	1,525	1,453	1,428	
Private services	5,933	6,261	6,600	6,769	
Self-employment	1,609	1,947	1,886	1,886	
Central and local government	4,078	4,888	5,337	5,300	
Unemployed	281	575	1,332	1,450	
Market-sector workers available to support each government-employed or unemployed worker	4.7	3.7	2.9	2.9	(2.2)

Source: *National Income and Expenditure*, Table 1.11, and *Department of Employment Gazette* and *Annual Abstract of Statistics*. The 1987 market-sector employment estimate is based on the assumption that the trend of 1966-73 continues until 1987.

The market sector of the economy has to support both the public services provided by central and local government and the unemployed. When the latter are added, it can be seen how rapidly the burden on the market sector has grown in Britain. In 1966 there were 20,707,000 market sector workers to support 4,359,000 through the taxes, etc., that they paid. By the start of the world recession the situation had deteriorated—there were 625,000 fewer market sector workers to support 1,104,000 more workers who were either unemployed or in central and local government. Throughout the world recession the situation has, of course, deteriorated further, as in most other countries. By 1977 there were less than three market sector workers to support each unemployed or government worker, as against 4.7 in 1966. Whether a worker is unemployed or in central and local government, he must be supported through the taxes paid by workers in agriculture, industry, commerce, transport, communications, the private services and self-employment.

118

Towards 1987: growth in non-market sector

An even more worrying situation arises if the figures are extrapolated to 1987. To begin with, it is generally agreed that the British labour force will increase by about a million in the next 10 years. Demographic change is now favouring growth in the labour force. Suppose the market sector of the economy stays on trend and drops another 785,000 jobs in 1977-87: Britain will then reach a situation where there are only 2.2 workers producing something for sale to support everyone who is unemployed or in the public services. This figure can be arrived at very simply. If there are going to be $27\frac{1}{2}$ million workers in 1987, and roughly 19 million are selling their output, there will be $8\frac{1}{2}$ million left who will either be employed in the public services or unemployed. Either way they will need support from the taxpayer.

It is scarcely necessary to remind an IEA Seminar what will happen if these workers are not supported by taxation. John Maynard Keynes's analysis of the German hyper-inflation of 1922-23 was especially acute; he explained in his *Tract on Monetary Reform* that if government expenditure is not financed through the taxation of incomes or capital, it will be financed through the taxation of cash balances instead.[1] The bulk of the government deficit is financed by printing money which raises prices, and then the government is in effect taxing everyone who is holding a building society deposit, or a bank account of any kind, for they all have less real purchasing power. The public sector then gets the extra purchasing power it requires at the expense of holders of deposits denominated in money. But this is the most chaotic way of all of financing the non-market sector. If Britain reaches a situation by 1987 where there are only 2.2 market sector workers to support everyone who is either unemployed or in government service, the country is bound to require far higher rates of taxation than it has had before—which is saying something—or far more of the government sector will be financed through the Keynesian mechanism of taxing cash balances which would produce accelerating inflation and ultimately hyper-inflation.

There is one final point to note about Table 1. In the way that the arithmetic is presented, it makes no difference whether the $8\frac{1}{2}$ million who will not be employed in the market sector by 1987 are

---

[1] J. M. Keynes, *A Tract on Monetary Reform*, London, 1924, Chapter II: 'Inflation as a Method of Taxation'.

in central or local government or unemployed. It is a 2.2 ratio either way. It is a little more expensive to support them if they are teachers or social workers, but the extra cost of supporting them in work is becoming less each year in relation to the cost of supporting them out of work. They will have to be supported, and there will by 1987 be only a little over two people working to produce something for sale to support each one who is not if present trends continue.

So the lesson clearly is that the drop of 785,000 in market sector employment from 1977 to 1987 must not happen. If it does, it is easy to see that unemployment will rise to over three million if government employment is held at 5.3 million, and still rise to two million if government employment is allowed to grow by another million. That is why extra job creation in the public sector is simply a palliative. It does not alter the fundamental ratio that there will be only two producers of marketed output to finance each non-producer of marketed output. Only the creation of extra market sector jobs can influence this fundamental ratio, but how does one expand the market sector?

Expanding the market sector
The problem cannot be solved through the expansion of the private services alone. As Table 1 shows, the private services and the self-employed expanded by 1,113,000 in 1966-77, and can be expected to go on increasing. The proportion of the labour force in the service sector is higher by about 10 per cent in Canada and the United States than in Europe. The income elasticity of demand for services is higher than one; as society becomes richer, resources move on balance into the service sector. But Britain is still at an intermediate stage where the labour force is hungry for extra manufactures, and the manufactures which people rushed to buy as soon as they got an extra 7 per cent of real disposable income in 1978, came very largely from abroad. So there is no doubt that, as Britain expands (and all will hope that expansion will continue) towards Canadian and United States living standards, in the first instance it is extra manufactures that people will wish to buy, and it is therefore extra manufactures that the country ought to be capable of producing. Otherwise the extra demand and the extra real incomes that accompany growth will go not into Britain's own manufacturing sector but into imports. So the industrial employment trend is in fact vital. Britain must therefore halt or at least slow down de-industrialisation for the loss of

1,087,000 industrial jobs in the seven years immediately before the world recession is too fast.

How? A most interesting Harvard-MIT study arrived at the result that, throughout North America, 57 per cent of all industrial jobs are lost each decade as a result of international competition, the obsolescence of plant, and the development of new products.[2] An equivalent number of industrial jobs is on balance created, but predominantly in the South of the United States where taxation is lower than in the Galbraithian North-East, wage-costs are lower and unions are weaker. In the North-East jobs are on balance lost because far fewer new ones are created than the 57 per cent that disappear. In the South, jobs are on balance gained on a substantial scale. In other parts of the United States the combined effects of job loss and job creation in industry are approximately neutral. One must see economic progress in these terms, as the West German and Japanese papers by Professor Watrin and Professor Okano emphasise. In Japan, 20 per cent of shipbuilding jobs were lost in four years —and replaced by good ones elsewhere. A country can progress only by putting in good jobs at the top end—by moving up-market. There is no doubt that the 57 per cent will be lost, whatever they are.

This is where the argument reaches the second British palliative now fashionable in trade union circles and elsewhere. Much British thinking, quoted by Dr Addison, and written about recently by Mr David Basnett,[3] favours job subsidies, job preservation and work sharing. This is all an attempt to stop the 57 per cent of jobs from disappearing. It can be only temporary and is bound to become increasingly expensive. The solution must be to create extra jobs at the top end. Again, how?

The product cycle in international trade
A slight digression will be introduced here, which is extremely germane to the Japanese and West German experience. There is a

---

[2] The results of this research at the Harvard-MIT Joint Center for Urban Studies by a team led by David L. Birch and Peter Allaman are outlined in the article, 'Business Loves the Sunbelt (and *Vice Versa*)', by G. Breckenfeld, *Fortune*, June 1977.

[3] David Basnett, 'North Sea Oil—A Chance to Tackle Unemployment', *Lloyds Bank Review*, October 1978.

very interesting development in international trade theory on the relevance of the product cycle. When a country introduces a successful new product it has monopoly power in it, and the country is able to charge a very high price in relation to its costs, it finds its sale extremely profitable, and obviously for the orthodox this produces a large comparative advantage in international trade. After a few years some countries start to make that product under licence; other countries produce imitations; those with much lower wage costs per unit start to manufacture it. Result: it ceases to be hyper-profitable. It then becomes a perfectly ordinary product which has to be sold overseas against strong international competition—and it faces equal international competition in home markets. So the real advantages in international trade go to the countries that can come *first* in the product cycle.

But it must be a successful product—a Comet or a Concorde will not do.[4] The Germans and the Japanese have a much better record than the British of coming *first* in the product cycle, which depends on high expenditures on marketing and research and development as well as on capital investment to manufacture new products, all of which require cash flow. Companies will economise in research and development and marketing where they are short of cash. Yet such economies all sacrifice future cash flows for the sake of present profitability. The cash flows of British companies have been under exceptional pressure so it will not be surprising if they have spent less than international competitors on the development of new products.

---

[4]M. V. Posner, 'International Trade and Technical Change', *Oxford Economic Papers*, October 1961; G. C. Hufbauer, *Synthetic Materials and the Theory of International Trade*, Duckworth, 1965; R. Vernon, 'International Investment and International Trade in the Product Cycle', *Quarterly Journal of Economics*, 1966; W. Gruber, D. Mehta and R. Vernon, 'The R & D Factor in International Trade and International Investment in United States Industries', *Journal of Political Economy*, 1967; and H. G. Johnson, *Comparative Cost and Commercial Policy Theory for a Developing World Economy*, Wicksell Lectures, Almquist and Wicksell, Stockholm, 1968.

TABLE 2

PROFITABILITY OF BRITISH INDUSTRIAL AND
COMMERCIAL COMPANIES: RATIOS OF GDP,
1967 TO 1977

	Gross trading profits	Net of capital consumption, stock appreciation and taxation	Including interest, rent and foreign income received, and deducting interest paid
	%	%	%
1967-71	14.8	7.6	7.5
1973	15.2	5.0	5.2
1975	12.5	3.4	2.2
1976	13.3	3.3	3.0
1977	13.7	4.4	3.6

Source: *National Income and Expenditure*, 1967-77.

Table 2 shows that British net company cash flows have fallen by well over one-half as a share of the National Income since the not especially prosperous period of 1967-71. So if moving up-market is the solution to the problem, how are British companies to do this with only half the net cash flows of the late 1960s? Professor Fisher demonstrated that the first-best solution to Britain's problem is undoubtedly a restoration of company profitability. There is indeed no way of putting the situation right without a considerable advance in company profitability. But this requires either a reduction in wages without a reduction in productivity, or higher productivity. Reducing real wages in British conditions has been tried, for a brief time in 1975-77, but real wages have now more than made good the ground lost then. On raising productivity, Professor Rees gave a beautiful account—which could be squared and cubed in terms of British unions—to explain the negative union attitudes to raising productivity in the United States.

Britain in a trap
So Britain is in a trap. The country cannot have the first-best solution —to restore company profitability in order to go up-market—because productivity cannot be raised substantially, given union resistance. And it is also impossible to cut real wages. What is Britain to do? While British governments have a terrible record when it comes to choosing successful future projects, if the analysis points to the

necessity to go up-market, the country must surely consider seriously the possibility of using government finance to assist the private sector of the economy.

Government record of waste
It should not be relied upon lightly. Governments have an extraordinary record of waste in public sector spending. Fifteen years ago economists were a little prone to regard the private sector of economies as full of inefficiencies and departures from Pareto optimum conditions which each called for intervention. At the same time they regarded those who ran the public sector as all-knowing, capable of taking both private and social costs into account, and therefore likely to take perfect decisions. This has led Professor Flores of the University of Madrid to remark that:

> 'The private sector can be defined as the part of the economy that the government controls: the public sector is the part that nobody controls.'

What Professor Flores describes has been happening in a number of countries, including Britain. Sir Ieuan Maddock, Chief Scientist at the Department of Industry from 1974 to 1977, pointed out in his Royal Society lecture of 1975 that nuclear power was, at the height of the nuclear energy programme, 'costing the nation some $2\frac{1}{2}$ per cent of its GNP' to supply 'under 3 per cent of the total energy consumption' in recent years. There are many similar cases in Britain and other countries. In 1975 the British public corporations needed loans or subsidies of 58 pence for every pound's worth of net output they produced.[5]

The British public sector has an appalling record of spending money indiscriminately. There are echoes in the papers by Dr Addison and Professor Fisher of the relevance of this for job creation. What are the chances that the public sector can do better than the private sector which it seeks to control? With Rolls-Royce it has clearly achieved a success, and this shows that success is a possibility. Without government financial support, the Rolls-Royce Aero Division would not now exist, and the company now stands a chance of obtaining up to 30 per cent of the world market for the kinds of engine in which it is an international leader in the product cycle. If

---

[5] Walter Eltis, 'The True Deficits of the Public Corporations', *Lloyds Bank Review*, January 1979.

company cash flows are inadequate to finance the research and development necessary to lead in the product cycle, ought any government to spurn the idea of providing help when leadership in the product cycle is so important? In the early stages of the Japanese and French economic miracles, public money did go in these directions.

The Keynesian solution?

What are the other possibilities for government policy, because no-one is going to be especially hopeful that the Department of Industry will make better judgements in the next 10 years than it made in the last 10? First, what about Keynesian policy? Can Britain, using North Sea oil, engineer a boom that will raise cash flows to produce a Keynesian boom of the kind Professor Fisher did not favour, in order to encourage and permit the private sector of the economy to raise its investment and in the process also further research and development, product improvement, product promotion, and so on? Clearly, if Britain can expand its economy, more economic resources will flow in the directions that can contribute to exports and employment, and North Sea oil will produce a far better balance of payments than Britain had when the Keynesian card was last played.

The difficulty with these policies at the moment is that the Keynesians have lost their multiplier. There seems no doubt that, for the industrial sector of the economy, the import ratio is currently around 35 per cent. The income elasticity of demand for imported manufactures is at least two and perhaps not far short of three. The effect is that Britain has a marginal propensity to import manufactured goods of at least 70 per cent, that is, at least 70 per cent of any increase in demand for manufactures that results from the Keynesian expansion of the economy now appears to be met from overseas. Hence such demand as the government creates does not have the multiplier effects it has in Keynesian text-books. It is presumably because they want to keep these books in print that the Keynesians now need import controls. That is one way of preserving their multiplier. Converting the world to Keynesian expansionism is, of course, another, but the West Germans with $2\frac{1}{2}$ per cent inflation, $3\frac{1}{2}$ per cent unemployment and 4 per cent interest rates show no sign of wishing to learn any economics from Cambridge, England. Hence, Britain and Samuelson-educated North America had to pursue their recent bursts of deficit-financed Keynesian expansion unaccompanied by most of the rest of the world, which produced payments deficits for the English-reading countries, a falling dollar, and Britain's apparently negligible multiplier.

The monetarist solution?

If the Keynesians have so little to offer to assist in the solution of the employment problem, what contribution, if any, can the monetarists make? Several papers have emphasised that Keynesian policies are liable to take the economy erratically towards a full-employment ceiling where expansion has to cease. They did not use the term 'full-employment ceiling', but referred instead to the situation where 'inflation starts to accelerate rapidly'. Now one of the more convincing pieces of economic analysis in the past decade has been the monetarists' 'natural rate of unemployment',[6] defined so that inflation accelerates where unemployment is less than the 'natural' rate and decelerates where it exceeds the 'natural' rate. When Mr Heath brought unemployment down below a million in 1972-73, inflation accelerated massively. When Mr Callaghan lifted unemployment to a million-and-a-half, inflation started to decelerate. If this theoretical approach is valid, the critical unemployment rate is nowadays around a million-and-a-half. It used to be 500,000 or less.

There are several obvious explanations for this increase in the 'natural' rate of unemployment of around a million. Their devastating effect has been that unemployment has had to be about a million higher than it used to be (with employment therefore one-and-a-half million or so lower since not all the unemployed register) whenever governments have sought to curb accelerating inflation. One reason for the dramatic rise in the 'natural' rate of unemployment is that there have been two important changes in trade union law. Secondary picketing has become legal so that, when one group of workers strikes, others in no way involved in the dispute can be prevented from working. This increases the probability that a strike will succeed. And the legalisation of the closed shop has had the effect that workers who wish to end a strike can be told: 'You will never work again', because expulsion from a union of anyone who breaks

---

[6] Milton Friedman, 'The Role of Monetary Policy', *American Economic Review*, 1968; and Milton Friedman and David Laidler, *Unemployment versus Inflation?*, Occasional Paper 44, IEA, London, 1975.

the solidarity of a strike can destroy his livelihood. In the absence of strike ballots, minorities can start strikes that the majority cannot end.

These developments all increase the probability that strikes will be called, even when unemployment is high, and that they will be pushed through until large increases in money wages are obtained. They will therefore all increase the 'natural' rate of unemployment, and therefore the unemployment that governments must maintain when striving to keep inflation under control.

The legalisation of secondary picketing and the closed shop are recent and may well have played a part in the increase in the 'natural' rate of unemployment from half-a-million to one-and-a-half million. Strike ballots were, of course, only briefly compulsory so their abandonment cannot be blamed for the long-term deterioration in the situation.

The role of social security benefits
A very significant change that has occurred since the early 1960s when the 'natural' rate of unemployment was half-a-million or so is the very large increase in the ratio of social security benefits to average earnings less tax. Whatever this ratio may be for the average worker, it has risen very significantly: the unemployed now receive between one-third and one-half more than they used to in the early 1960s relatively to the net-of-tax earnings of those at work. It is therefore straightforward economic analysis that the cost of 'searching' for better-paid work, either by going on strike or by changing employers has been much reduced. No wonder that an extra million workers are searching for better-paid work than in the 1950s and the early 1960s, and that they are more prepared to use the strike weapon, even if it threatens the bankruptcy of their companies and the ending of their present jobs. They can then *afford* to search for other work which will pay them the wages they seek.

The suggestion that the 'natural' rate of unemployment has risen by about a million fits, at any rate superficially, what Lord Kaldor used to call 'the stylised facts', which indicates that it may be impossible to cut the level of unemployment in Britain without an equivalent fall in the 'natural' rate of unemployment. If successful job-creation actually resulted from the discovery of numerous product-cycle-leaders by the Department of Industry, or if there were successful Keynesian expansion, it would lead to accelerating inflation as soon as unemployment fell below the now massive 'natural' rate. That may be exactly what has happened since the summer of 1978. This must then lead to the reversal of the successful job-creation policies at the very moment that they begin to bring unemployment down. Any policy to raise employment is thus bound to produce only superficial and shortlived results if it fails to bring the 'natural' rate of unemployment down.

Reducing the 'natural' rate of unemployment

How? The legislation on trade unions can be reversed. There is no controversy about the desirability of policies to increase labour mobility through retraining and flexibility in the housing market. The nettle is the relative incomes of the employed and the unemployed and the relative incomes of people in work and those on strike because, in terms of the normal economic analysis of the price mechanism, if it costs relatively little to be on strike or unemployed, more people are going to be willing to strike or to be unemployed, and it will therefore require more unemployment to stabilise the labour market.

There are obviously constraints on the possible freedom of action of government, and it may well be that it is politically impractical (and it would also do obvious social damage) to reduce significantly the financial support for the unemployed. It could create severe social tension. The alternative way of dealing with the difficulty, to increase the real take-home pay of those at work, which Mr Callaghan and Mr Healey appeared at one time to favour for a few months, may have potential. The practical approach to the high 'natural' rate of unemployment in British circumstances may be to cut average and marginal tax rates for the ordinary worker. The central argument is that, from the point of view of restoring the economics of the labour market, marginal taxation must be cut at the lower end if a significant differential between people at work and those searching for work is to be restored.

Reducing government expenditure

To return to the previous argument, this obviously means that the government expenditure ratio must be cut because workers' taxation cannot be brought down through a larger budget deficit. Britain's deficit already exceeds what can be afforded if the stability of the economy and the currency is to be maintained. So, to return to Table

1, to produce a significant potential for tax cuts, the ratio of tax-paying market-sector employment must be raised substantially relatively to tax-using employment in central and local government and the requirements of the unemployed.

This solution emphasises the trap Britain is in. To restore incentives to work in the ordinary labour market, taxation, and therefore government expenditure, must be cut. To achieve market-sector expansion the 'natural' rate of unemployment must be reduced, but one of the main policies to achieve this end cannot be implemented until the market sector has already started to expand, because it is only then that the country will be able to cut taxation really substantially for the average worker.

Britain is thus in a vicious circle from which it is extremely difficult to break out. What becomes clear is that we may have to be content at first with small steps in the right direction. The *first* small step will be to slim government expenditure wherever this can be achieved— and it is now known that real government spending was reduced by more than 7 per cent between fiscal 1976-77 and fiscal 1977-78, mainly as a result of the extensive use of 'cash limits'.[7] There are always a number of dispensable items in government expenditure, and it is vital to the country that spending be cut quickly by 3, 4, 5 or 6 per cent so that a start can be made towards getting taxation down at the lower end of the scale.

Second, it is vital that the government try to find more subsidies of the Rolls-Royce kind to help British industry to move up-market and arrest the trend of de-industrialisation from which the country has suffered. This is a claim on the resources saved by cutting 'public' expenditure elsewhere, but like tax cuts it can assist the expansion of the market sector from which future tax revenues will be ultimately derived.

Third, the country must not return to Heath-type policies of severe price controls in industry, which cut industrial cash flows so drastically in the early 1970s and made it especially difficult for private industry to move up-market. The massive rise in import penetration since then is not unassociated with the weaknesses in industrial cash flow which have forced many British firms down-market.

---

[7] *The Government's Expenditure Plans, 1979-80 to 1982-83*, Cmnd. 7439, HMSO, London, January 1979, p. 3.

Finally, it must be recognised that the private services increased their employment by over a million between 1966 and 1977, that they are necessarily the most dynamic sector of the economy in a rich society, and that the government should do nothing to restrict their expansion.

To sum up, the situation will be wholly satisfactory only when the country manages both to cut the 'natural' rate of unemployment and to restore the expansion of employment in the market sector. These together will permit expansion in output and employment which would finance the rise in living standards and the improvements in social services that the country so obviously desires.

Questions and Discussion

RALPH HARRIS (*Chairman*): Thank you, Mr Eltis, for your luminously clear exposition. I suspect it will provoke a lot of questions and comments. I reflected while you were speaking that the only time in the whole of to-day's conference on job creation that the term 'full employment' has been used was when you said that no-one had so far used the 'full employment ceiling' as a concept.

PROF. ALBERT REES: I am about to do something outrageous! I am going to defend John Maynard Keynes at an IEA meeting—it may be the last one I am ever invited to! Both Professor Fisher and Mr Eltis have criticised that portion of *The General Theory* in which Keynes discusses the downward rigidity of money wages and the question of wage relativity. I happen to think that that portion of *The General Theory* is, perhaps, indeed correct and has to be reckoned with. And I base this contention, at least for the United States, on direct experience administering incomes policy for three or four years, and for the UK, where I have less direct experience, largely on the writings about wage relativities by Professor Henry Phelps Brown.

What Keynes says is that workers will tolerate a cut in real wages if it comes *via* a rise in the price level and not if it comes *via* a fall in the money wage. And the reason he gives is, very simply, that a fall in the money wage can never be accomplished uniformly throughout the economy, so that in the process of cutting money and wages you are always changing wage relativities, which workers will resist, whereas a rise in prices is uniform and therefore will be resisted much less fiercely and perhaps much more slowly. The United States had a drop of about 3 per cent in real wages across the board at the time of the Arab oil boycott. Real resources had to be exported in order to pay for imported petroleum without which our economy will not run. Workers stood for that but would not have stood for it if it had been done on the money wage side. Now I also accept Professor Fisher's observation this morning that, over the long run, relative wages change. They respond to market forces but very slowly; and they respond in an asymetrical way in that, if a set of relative wages is wrong, the only way you can go about putting it right in the kind of economy we have in modern industrial nations is to raise the money wage of those whose relative wage is too low. You cannot do it the other way round.

To anyone who questions this assertion I propose that you undertake an experiment. Suppose you employ someone, let us say a secretary or a research assistant, and you go to this secretary and tell her that you are pleased to announce that starting next Monday her wages will be raised by £2 a week: she will be very happy. And then after you have observed her happiness, tell her 'Oh, by the way, everyone else's wages but yours have been raised by £3 a week'. She will not only be less happy than after the first message but she will be less happy than she was to begin with. I submit that there are many people who would rather not have an increase at all than have an increase of £2 if everyone else gets £3. In designing our policy that is a force we have to reckon with, and that it is a rather profound insight of Keynes, because he was not a labour economist. I think it puts impediments in the way of certain policies that we would like to propose so that we will have to be clever in doing some things that need to be done in rather indirect ways.

JOHN WOOD (*IEA*): As Walter Eltis said, I am sure that 1966 is the great watershed for employment. If you look at the trend over the whole period before and after, it is from that moment onwards that you have this extraordinary decline in the labour force to which he has drawn our attention, and also you seem to have a difference in kind rather than degree in the amount of unemployment. Indeed, Walter Eltis has pointed out there is a partial explanation of that phenomenon because in the same year, 1966, we changed our arrangements for unemployment support in Britain. Up to 1966, the total cost to government of unemployment support had hardly ever been up to £100 million in a year. Then we changed these arrangements and it very rapidly went up. By 1974 it was £500 million and I think, although I have not looked at the figures recently, it is something of the order of about £1,300 million now. So there has been this increase in the demand for unemployed people and a response.

JOHN BURTON (*Kingston Polytechnic*): Professor Rees said he agreed with the Keynesian analysis that a balanced deflation is impossible because it will alter the structure of re ative wages, whereas a balanced

131

inflation would leave differentials unchanged. Now I would put it to Professor Rees that this contrast is quite incorrect. All inflation changes the structure of relative prices, and relative wages as well, because we do not live in a world of helicopter money where helicopters come over and uniformly paper people with money. Money always enters the economy through particular channels and will always change the structure of relative prices and relative wages depending upon where the Government is spending the money from its budget deficit. You get exactly the same problem with a deflation. With an inflation as with a deflation, it will always change the structure of relative prices and wages. The central flaw in Keynes's economics is that he did not realise that deficiency. It was too aggregative in every sense. If we want to understand the impact of de-flation/inflation, which *always* alters the structure of relative prices and wages, we have to go over to the Hayekian analysis of inflation put forward in 1931.

PROF. MALCOLM R. FISHER: It seems to me that rational skilled men must be terribly upset by the squeeze imposed on skill differentials which Mr Heath, I believe, inaugurated in Phase Two of the incomes and prices policy in 1972 and has been imposed frequently around the world since. Governments, on Keynesian advice, are evidently responsible in this way for transmitting so much unhappiness.

I rise really in connection with Walter Eltis's paper. Leaving my political petticoat showing a little, I am uneasy about his notion of governments rendering subsidies to the private sector. I am not abolutely *au fait* with the Rolls-Royce story, but at face value his argument seems to imply that, given the alternative ways in which government can subsidise, this way has a good deal going for it. If you think about it, this is not very different from the discussion on international trade in the literature, which goes right back to 'infant industry' subsidies or tariffs as opposed to other forms of subsidy or tariff. There is a continuity in the literature, so we are simply going back, as it were, to where we came in. In the context of Britain today, we might ask why we should be so keen on the government sector en-couraging the Rolls-Royce type of activity? If Walter Eltis has a case, it seems to be in terms of the earlier part of his lecture that government is so busy strangulating and regulating the private economy that the financial system of the private economy has lost all confidence to lend in anticipation of profit. Since the private sector now lacks the resilience to further new development, the Government has to step in to fill the gap.

WALTER ELTIS: On Professor Rees's point, I do not think there is any disagreement that real wages have to be cut in certain situations to maintain or to raise employment. I personally would not disagree with the view that you cut real wages by raising prices instead of by cutting money wages.

What I want to do now is to give you a figure on the British bounceback. From 1964 to 1969, real net earnings in Britain rose (in 1963 prices, net of all deductions) from £15.65 to £16.19. In other words, during that period of five years, the workers exercised immense patience in agreeing to accept increases of 2, 3, 4 per cent in price-controlled, wage-controlled agreements of all kinds and the share of consumption by workers in the national income fell drastically. The effect of this, shall we say, Keynesian willingness to go along with incomes policy and accept a large fall in real wages in relation to productivity was that many British unions elected militants who used the bargaining powers that were already latent in their position. So between 1969 and 1973—in fact one could go on to 1975—the British worker was no longer squeezable. He had organised himself so that the share of workers' consumption in the national income could be made larger. There was nothing any Keynesian could do to stop him and the result was that the increase in government spending during that period was entirely at the expense of profits and the balance of payments. This is a kind of illustration—it can obviously be no more than an illustration—of what I understand to be Professor Fisher's view, which I share, that you cannot hold the workers' real wages down for long by such tinkering devices.

Turning to Professor Fisher and the Rolls-Royce subsidy, I think the economic concept that I would propose is that of externalities. Taking the view that being early in the product cycle and maintaining our share of world trade is important—and remember Rolls-Royce used to power half the world's civil airliners—Rolls-Royce now has a chance of capturing 35 per cent of the market in the next generation. But Rolls-Royce would have disappeared as an aero-engine producer without government subsidy at the time when the market was not prepared to give it twopence. We would have lost that potential 35 per cent which we may now get.

The externality comes in like this. If we are early in the product cycle and hold our share of world trade, this allows industry and commerce to expand at a faster rate than it otherwise would. It therefore finances more social services and so on. So if there is a balance of payments constraint and if devaluation—and I am sure we would agree on this—is not an adequate way of dealing with it, anything that relieves the balance-of-payments constraint does have significant externalities for the rest of the community, which justifies subsidy. The danger is, of course, that the subsidy will do no good whatsoever and simply go to the government's friends.

JOHN LEWIS (*Cross Keys College*): It seems that most speakers have agreed that we have to lower real wages, for a while at any rate, and that it will be easier to do so by raising prices than by attempting to attack wages directly. I would have thought the easiest way to do that would be a direct trade-off between an increase in VAT and a cut in the standard rate of income tax.

My main complaint is nothing has been said so far on the development about which we hear so much talk, a lot of it no doubt exaggerated, namely the impact of silicon chips or micro-processors. Even allowing for all the exaggeration, it is going to destroy a great many jobs over the next few years and I wonder whether any of the speakers or others would afford us observations on this rather important matter.

DR BARRY BRACEWELL-MILNES: On Mr Eltis's interesting address, I wanted to make the same criticism that Professor Fisher raised. Having heard Mr Eltis's answer to Professor Fisher, I feel my original objection has redoubled force. We went through all this stuff about externalities years ago with Kaldor and Selective Employment Tax (SET). I cannot see that Mr Eltis is putting before us anything more convincing than what we heard on the subject of SET in 1966, and all the arguments for increasing the growth of the economy, which was the aim in those days, by giving special treatment to the manufacturing industry sector. To generalise a little, Mr Eltis made the excellent point that it is of no consequence how you divide the figures between central and local government on the one side and the unemployed on the other—they are all equally a burden on the productive sector. To complement that, I would contend that it is of no consequence how you divide the productive sector between the manufacturing and industrial wing on the one side and the services wing on the other.

NOEL PICARDA-KEMP (*Union of Independent Companies*): Adrian Berry, the Science Correspondent of the *Daily Telegraph*, has written a very fanciful book about how matter in space disappears into black holes and (I think) re-emerges in white stars. I wonder if the speaker might agree there is a lesson here for us in industry? At the moment we have locked into failing industries both money in the form of subsidies to keep jobs going and workers who refuse to leave to go to new industries where opportunities might exist. The reason is that, if they stick with it to the end, they get a very large settlement in the form of redundancy pay. This is now becoming an alarming problem for job mobility. I wonder if there is any advice you can give and if you think there might be something to be said for requiring companies in receipt of job creation or preservation subsidies from the state, to exclude the workers from the provisions of legislation giving them protection in the form of redundancy payments?

E. G. WHYBREW (*Department of Employment*): I have a great deal of sympathy for a number of the things Walter Eltis has said. Many of his policy prescriptions I find it easy to go along with, for example, his views on panaceas, and on the view that work sharing is no solution unless you get income sharing as well. Equally, it is not a solution to talk about mopping up unemployment by creating permanent jobs in the public sector.

One of the things that worried me about Walter Eltis's presentation was that it seemed to concentrate a great deal on maintaining employment or increasing employment in the market sector, which I would have thought we were doing now. Again I do not expect many in this audience to disagree with the statement that we will only get out of our present difficulties when we have an efficient wealth-creating sector, and I do not think that necessarily means a wealth-creating sector which employs more people. One of my worries about the presentation is that it was done initially in employment terms. I think there is a danger in doing that. When the industrial strategy was launched, a larger number of people saw it as a means of stopping de-industrialisation, by which they meant stopping any form of unemployment in the manufacturing sector. I am not sure that is really what Walter Eltis is suggesting but I do think he is subject to that misinterpretation.

WALTER ELTIS: I think Ted Whybrew's point is fundamental and one I can hardly deal with in a minute or two. My position would be that there are really two things on which we ought to focus attention. In the first place, are there many examples of countries which have managed to raise productivity in stagnant markets when raising productivity means losing jobs? The ideal situation (and I am sure this was the situation in Japan when they achieved such startling success) is when the market sector of the economy is in what is in every way a positive sum game. In other words, when you are raising profits, raising real wages, raising employment, there is a view that the employers and the workers are all on the same side. They are all gaining, and all they are bargaining about is how the gains are to be shared between them. You then have very equable trade unions. But if you are facing an extremely low growth rate and—as in the case of *The Times* and the *Sunday Times*—you are trying to raise productivity to 30 per cent or whatever it is, then it is very hard to negotiate because you are offering the workers a plus and a minus: more pay and less jobs. And so higher productivity is absolutely essential, but I think we can get it only if we restore an environment of growth. Now with the figures that I put up, the situation was not looking too bad between 1967 and 1976, and Ted Whybrew would know more about the 1978 figures, but I would guess that when we compare 1978 with 1979 we are going to have some more pleasant surprises. We are now witnessing growth, we are in a positive sum game because taxation is coming down. We can therefore hope to raise productivity.

Secondly, I tend to think of productivity in terms of better products rather than producing the same products more cheaply because this is what is so crucial internationally. In other words, if the same labour force can produce something that can be sold at a higher international price because it is better designed, that is an increase in productivity. And so I think the vital thing which I tried to emphasise was the necessity to go up market, both by raising productivity and by improving designs, and so on.

Finally, there is one point where I do not go along with Ted Whybrew. Supposing in some future Utopia we manage to produce all the goods and services we need with just 10 per cent of the country's labour. If 10 per cent work in the market sector producing all the goods and services we need and 90 per cent are in the non-market sector, we need a 90 per cent rate of taxation if we are to avoid hyper-inflation. It is hard enough to run an economy with an average share of taxation of 43 per cent or whatever it is that we have, and the thought of having to go from 43 to 90 per cent as we achieve this new Utopia simply horrifies me. I think as we move towards this Utopia we might find ourselves having to do dreadful things like marketing education and health! We might want to spend 70 per cent of our resources on education, health, pensions and so on, but we cannot possibly do that by taxation because 70, 80, 90 per cent share of taxation is impractical. We would at some point, I suspect, have to live with a much smaller share of taxation. So taxation matters if people mind about taxation, and then it does matter whether services are supplied through the market sector or the non-market sector.

On silicon chips, my favourite remark was made by a distinguished businessman who said that the last economist he heard worrying about silicon chips was doubtless one who had been around when the wheel was invented and who would have produced a similar paper! There is no doubt that capital savings-type technical progress, which is what silicon chips are, offers a tremendous potential for higher productivity, and that there is no reason why we should not benefit from higher productivity by having faster growth and everything else we want. I do not think we ought to be frightened of higher productivity, and here I agree entirely with Professor Watrin.

Dr Bracewell-Milnes maintained services *versus* industry. I think that it is important to remember that productivity growth in private services is only around 1 per cent per annum. Therefore if all your growth is in private services, your growth rate is not going to exceed 1 per cent. Are your workers going to be content with a rate of growth of real wages of 1 per cent per annum? Manufacturing is the part of the economy where you can get growth rates of productivity of 3, 4, 5 per cent. Now in our final

Utopia, when almost everybody is in services, we shall have to approximate to a stationary state and workers will have to be so content with their Utopian position that they do not need wage increases. But at the moment people do want a rise in living standards, and we have all our growth occurring in a sector of the economy where there is only a 1 per cent productivity growth rate. That is a recipe for frustration. I agree wholly with what Mr Picarda-Kemp said about this business of firms closing down and that is extremely difficult. The newspaper reports often quote a worker as saying that if the company cannot pay proper wages, then it ought to go bankrupt. If 'proper wages' means a substantial margin on what you get when you are not working, and what you get when you are not working is too close to average earnings, then that method of thought would automatically bankrupt a high fraction of industry!

RALPH HARRIS: Thank you very much. I would like to end on a more cheerful note. Can I just ask, as an alternative to subsidising industry, what would be the effect of abolishing Corporation Tax in terms of cash flow for the company sector?

WALTER ELTIS: Extremely slight, I think. It is not really taxation, as everybody here knows, it is stock appreciation that is vital, and given the fact that British industry and commerce is extremely unprofitable, I doubt whether the taxation component would be more than 1 or 2 per cent. That would be my guess, but we still await the 1977 Blue Book.

RALPH HARRIS: Gentlemen, it is exactly 5 o'clock, and I am going to draw abruptly to an end. We have had a very full day, much illumination has been cast, still more will burst upon you when these papers are published in 1979, and it remains only for us to display our appreciation of our last speaker and all the previous speakers and other survivors who are still with us, and to congratulate ourselves on having lasted the course.

List of Participants at IEA Job Creation Seminar (*1st December 1978*)

ADDISON, DR JOHN, *Lecturer in Political Economy, University of Aberdeen*
ANDREWS-JONES, D. H., *Employee Relations Dept., Metal Box*
BAILEY, MICHAEL, *Economics Department, Rio Tinto-Zinc*
BARBACK, R. H., *Confederation of British Industry*
BARKER, GRAHAM, *Research Assistant, Confederation of British Industry*
BLACKWELL, JOHN, *Personnel Manager, East Midland Allied Press Limited*
BRACEWELL-MILNES, DR BARRY, *Erasmus University, Rotterdam*
BRIMLEY, W. J., *Taylor Woodrow*
BULLOCH, ANN, *Conservative Research Department*
BURTON, JOHN, *Principal Lecturer in Economics, Kingston Polytechnic*
BUTLER, DR EAMONN, *Adam Smith Institute*
BUTLER, DR STUART, *Adam Smith Institute*

CAIRNCROSS, FRANCES, *The Guardian*
CHIPLIN, BRIAN, *Department of Industrial Economics, Nottingham University*
CLARKE, PETER, *BBC Edinburgh*
COLOMBATTO, ENRICO, *Centro Einaudi, Turin*
COOK, K. W., *Director of Finance & Planning, Philips Industries*
CORR, JIM, *Policy Adviser to the then Prime Minister, Mr James Callaghan*

DIXON, J., *Department of Employment*

ELTIS, WALTER, *Exeter College, Oxford*
EYRES, STEPHEN, *News Editor, Free Nation*

FENN-SMITH, C. A. K., *M & G Group Limited*
FERRANTI, BASIL DE, *Ferranti Limited*
FISHER, PROFESSOR MALCOLM, *University of NSW, Australia*
FROST, GORDON, *Employee Relations Adviser, East Midland Allied Press Limited*

GERLACH, K., *University of Hanover*
GORTON, J. E., *BP Oil Limited*
GRIFFIN, W. T. J., *Chairman, GT Management*

HANKEY, J. B., *Tate & Lyle Refineries Limited*
HAYMAN, MISS A. C., *Central Policy Review Staff*
HENDERSON, RICHARD, *Sheppards & Chase*
HOOPER, NICK, *National Economic Development Office*

JACKSON, ROBERT, *Member of the European Parliament for Thames Valley*
JELLICOE, LORD
JOHNSON, PROFESSOR D., *Department of Economics & Banking, City of London Polytechnic*
JOHNSON, MRS EVA, *Rainier National Bank*
JOLLY, S. A., *Manager, Employee Relations, Personnel Department, Texaco Limited*

139

KELLERMAN, C., *New Business Manager, Tate & Lyle Refineries Limited*
KEMP, NOEL PICARDA, *Union of Independent Companies*

LANGTON, J. S., *Rolls-Royce Limited*
LAYARD, DR RICHARD, *London School of Economics*
LEWIS, JOHN, *Cross Keys College of Further Education, Gwent*
LEWIS, PETER, *Chairman, John Lewis Partnership*

MARGOLIS, CECIL, *North Yorkshire & Harrogate District Councils*
MEAKIN, J. C. H., *Director for Smaller Firms, Confederation of British Industry*
MENDEL, M. P., *Economist, BP Oil Limited*
MOULDING, TERRY, *Research & Policy Planning Department, Confederation of British Industry*

NUGENT, JIM, *Department of Economics, Kingston Polytechnic*

OKABE, MITSUAKI, *Bank of Japan*
OKANO, PROFESSOR YUKIHIDE, *Tokyo University (now St Antony's College, Oxford)*

PALAMOUNTAIN, EDGAR, *Managing Director, M & G Securities*
PETERS, ALAN, *Shell International*

RAU, NICHOLAS, *Department of Political Economy, University College, London*
REED, C. T., *C. Margolis (Harrogate) Limited*
REES, PROFESSOR ALBERT, *Princeton University, USA*
RICHARDS, GORDON, *Hammersmith & West London College*
ROBINSON, A. H., *Personnel Manager, Guardian Royal Exchange Assurance Limited*
RODMELL, BRIAN E., *Head of Economics Branch, Manpower Services Commission*
RYBURN, D. M., *Businessman*

SANDERS, PAUL P., *Economic Adviser, Commercial Union Assurance Co*
SANDERS, T. C., *Union of Independent Companies*
SAVIN, C. T., *Senior Policy Analyst, British Petroleum*
SHEPHERD, ROB, *Conservative Research Department*
SIEBERT, STANLEY, *Department of Economics, Stirling University*
SLOANE, PETER, *Department of Economics & Management, Paisley College, Paisley*
STEVENSON, R. B., *Market Intelligence Department, National Westminster Bank*
SYKES, A., *Willis Faber Limited*

VANDER ELST, PHILIP, *Journalist*
VERRY, DR DONALD, *Department of Political Economy, University College, London*

WASSELL, MARTIN, *International Chamber of Commerce*
WATRIN, PROFESSOR CHRISTIAN, *University of Cologne, West Germany*
WHYBREW, E. G., *Department of Employment*
WILKINS, DAVID, *Confederation of British Industry*
WOLFSON, MARK, *Hambros Bank*

Author Index

141

Subject Index

143

Some IEA Readings in Print

1. Education—A Framework for Choice
A. C. F. Beales, Mark Blaug, E. G. West, Sir Douglas Veale,
with an Appraisal by Dr Rhodes Boyson   2nd Edition 1970   (xvi + 100pp., 90p)

2. Growth through Industry
John Jewkes, Jack Wiseman, Ralph Harris, John Brunner, Richard Lynn, and
seven company chairmen   1967   (xiii + 157pp., £1·00)

4. Taxation—A Radical Approach
Vito Tanzi, J. B. Bracewell-Milnes, D. R. Myddelton   1970   (xii + 130pp., 90p)

7. Verdict on Rent Control
F. A. Hayek, Milton Friedman and George Stigler, Bertrand de Jouvenel, F. W. Paish,
Sven Rydenfelt, *with an Introduction by* F. G. Pennance 1972 (xvi + 80pp., £1·00)

9. The Long Debate on Poverty
R. M. Hartwell, G. E. Mingay, Rhodes Boyson, Norman McCord, C. G. Hanson,
A. W. Coats, W. H. Chaloner and W. O. Henderson, J. M. Jefferson
2nd Edition with an introductory essay by Norman Gash 1974 (xxxii + 243pp., £2·50)

10. Mergers, Take-overs, and the Structure of Industry
G. C. Allen, M. E. Beesley, Harold Edey, Brian Hindley, Sir Anthony Burney, Peter
Cannon, Ian Fraser, Lord Shawcross, Sir Geoffrey Howe, Lord Robbins
                                              1973   (ix + 92pp., £1·00)

11. Regional Policy For Ever?
Graham Hallett, Peter Randall, E. G. West   1973   (xii + 152pp., £1·80)

14. Inflation: Causes, Consequences, Cures
Lord Robbins, Samuel Brittan, A. W. Coats, Milton Friedman, Peter Jay, David Laidler
with an Addendum by F. A. Hayek 1974 3rd Impression 1976 (viii + 120pp., £2·00)

15. The Dilemmas of Government Expenditure
Robert Bacon and Walter Eltis, Tom Wilson, Jack Wiseman, David Howell, David
Marquand, John Pardoe, Richard Lynn   1976   (xi + 110pp., £2·00)

16. The State of Taxation
A. R. Prest, Colin Clark, Walter Elkan, Charles K. Rowley, Barry Bracewell-Milnes,
Ivor F. Pearce
Commentaries by Geoffrey E. Wood, Alun G. Davies, Nigel Lawson, T. W. Hutchison,
Alan T. Peacock, Michael Moohr, Malcolm R. Fisher, George Psacharopoulos,
Dennis Lees, J. S. Flemming, Douglas Eden *with an Address by* Lord Houghton
                                              1977   (xvi + 116pp., £2·00)

17. Trade Unions: Public Goods or Public 'Bads'?
Lord Robbins, Charles G. Hanson, John Burton, Cyril Grunfeld, Brian Griffiths,
Alan Peacock
Commentaries by Peter Mathias, Norman McCord, P. J. Sloane, J. T. Addison,
Martin Ricketts, George Yarrow, Charles T. Rowley, Dennis Lees, Harry Ferns,
Keith Hartley, Reg Prentice, Jo Grimond *with an Address by* Lord Scarman
                                              1978   (xiv + 134pp., £2·00)

18. The Economics of Politics
James M. Buchanan, Charles K. Rowley, Albert Breton, Jack Wiseman, Bruno Frey,
A. T. Peacock, Jo Grimond, W. A. Niskanen, Martin Ricketts
Commentaries by Nevil Johnson, Ken Judge, Henri Lepage, Robert Grant, Paul
Whiteley   1978   (xiii + 194pp., £3·00)

19. City Lights
E. Victor Morgan, R. A. Brealey, B. S. Yamey, Paul Bareau
                                              1979   (x + 70pp., £1·50)